Teaching GCSE Modern Languages

Teaching GCSE Modern Languages

Ewen Bird and Michael Dennison

HODDER AND STOUGHTON
LONDON SYDNEY AUCKLAND TORONTO

ISBN 0 340 408766

First published 1987

Typeset by Tradespools Ltd, Frome
Printed and bound in Great Britain for
Hodder and Stoughton Educational,
a division of Hodder and Stoughton Ltd,
Mill Road, Dunton Green, Sevenoaks, Kent,
by The Eastern Press, Reading and London

Contents

Acknowledgments

We wish to thank the many colleagues in Wiltshire schools whose informed criticism in lively debate on all aspects of the GCSE has helped us to formulate our opinions and ideas, for which we take full responsibility.

Bob Powell at the School of Education, University of Bath and Pat D'Arcy, English Adviser in Wiltshire, provided ideas for diagrams. We are also grateful for information contributed by Madeleine Davis, School of Education, Exeter University and by Allan Emmett, Assistant Secretary at the AEB.

We are indebted to Lesley Kendall and Yvonne Gough who, with great patience and good humour, coped with our scribble and transformed it into accurate typescript.

Finally, special thanks are due to close colleagues and family whose critical reading of the manuscript and many constructive suggestions gave great help. Without their support, this book would certainly have been the poorer.

Ewen Bird
Michael Dennison
March 1987

The authors and publishers would also like to thank the following for permission to reproduce examination questions and syllabus extracts in this book:
The Southern Examining Group, The Northern Examining Association, The Midland Examining Group, The London and East Anglian Group.

Introduction

It was suggested at a recent conference that, where a country had a nationally validated curriculum, a national system of examining at 16+ had little importance, since everyone knew what had been taught. Where, however, there is no nationally agreed curriculum, the need for testing becomes essential in order to validate across the country what has been learnt. Although there is now a discernible move towards central control, at present in the United Kingdom there is an emphasis on schools developing their own curricula without the prescription of this control; hence the expressed need to assess pupil performance at the end of their period of compulsory education.

The examination structure which evolved to meet this need was a two-tier one. The GCE and CSE division meant that the most able 20 per cent of pupils in each subject were considered suitable for examinations at O level and the next 40 per cent were expected to sit the CSE examinations. This left 40 per cent who were not expected to take any public examinations. In practice, however, well over 90 per cent of sixteen-year-olds took examinations in one or more subjects.

These examinations had long been criticised for their tendency to assess negatively, their emphasis on norm-referencing and on their bipartite nature within a largely non-selective system. Successive governments have sought a solution to these problems, and in 1984 the Secretary of State for Education announced that the existing examination system at 16+ was to be replaced by a single system to be called GCSE. This would mean that the nine O level and thirteen CSE boards were to be replaced by six GCSE examination boards or consortia. These are the Northern Examining Association, the Midland Examining Group, the London and East Anglian Group, the Southern Examining Group, the Welsh Joint Education Committee and the Northern Ireland Schools Examination Council. The Secondary Examinations Council (SEC) had already been set up to monitor all schemes and syllabuses and to ensure compliance with the national criteria.

At one stroke, the Secretary of State was introducing an element of conformity hitherto lacking in the examination structure. The main thrust of the new system was to be positive in its approach to assessment in order 'to show what pupils, know, understand and can do' (*General Criteria*).

The implications for modern languages have been considerable. In the past there had been a tendency for modern languages to be regarded as rather elitist. This derived from the way languages were traditionally taught, with an emphasis on translation and grammar manipulation. There existed in our modern-language departments a concern that pupils should acquire a knowledge of the code – the syntactical knowledge and manipulation of grammar required for a study of the forms of language. This, however, does not have a great deal to do with the practical skill of communication – as generations of ex-pupils have found to their cost when confronted with authentic language.

Research into the acquisition of foreign languages has shown that the ability to communicate does not depend entirely on an understanding of the linguistic code which is merely one facet of a more complex interaction. When language teaching is targeted towards communication skills, the code must be integrated into a pattern of work designed to improve pupil awareness of linguistic process, medium and product. Effective communication will only take place when all aspects of the foreign language have been integrated into a single programme. This may be expressed diagrammatically, as shown in Figure 1.

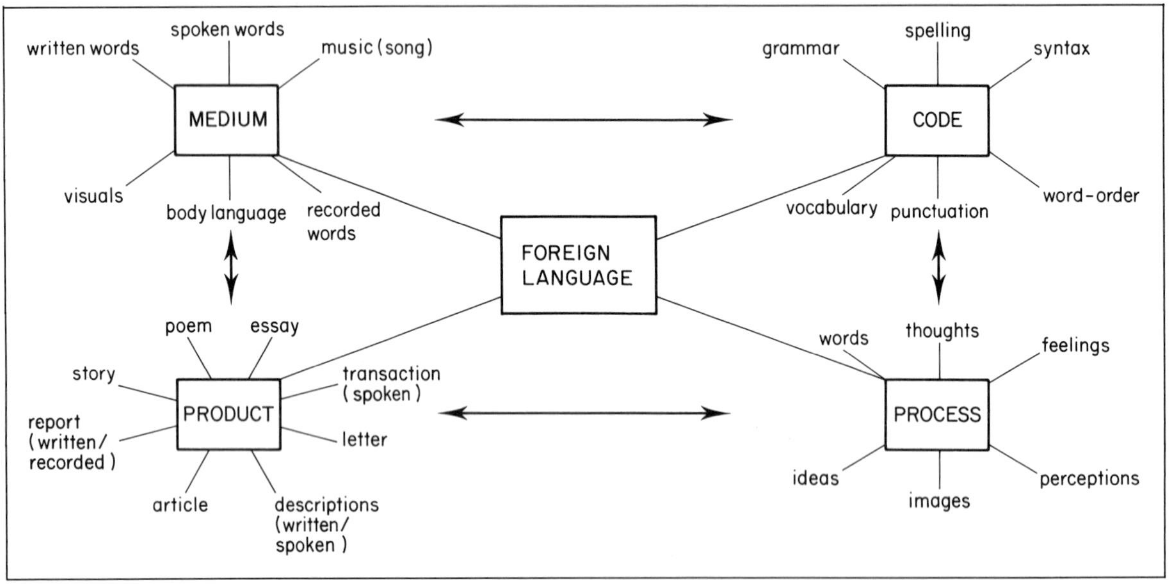

▲ *Fig. 1*

The principles guiding GCSE modern languages as set out in the *National Criteria – French* mirror this shift in emphasis from a study of the code towards the process and the product.

Pupils' motivation will improve when they are able to demonstrate positive achievements by communicating in the foreign language. The code is not forgotten but is only one, albeit essential, part of the communicative act. A more effective language course can be developed by directing pupils' attention, via process and product, to what can be understood and expressed.

This book demonstrates how the national criteria for modern languages have responded to these recent developments in the teaching of languages. Having explained the details of the

GCSE examination structure, the types of assessment and differences among the various consortia and syllabuses on offer, the book discusses the implications for classroom practice. It also shows how the teacher may incorporate the principles inherent in the national criteria into a teaching programme so that pupils are prepared more effectively for the demands of the GCSE examination. Finally it points to the future by suggesting some possible developments.

The GCSE examination, whatever faults it may have, represents a positive step forward for modern-language teaching. It provides an opportunity for major syllabus reform and a change in attitude. This is a situation which occurs but rarely and we most exploit it fully.

I The national criteria

A CONTEXT FOR CHANGE

There is a hope, pious or otherwise, amongst many language teachers that national criteria and a more precisely defined examination syllabus will have a positive and beneficial effect on language teaching. It is indeed stated in the *National Criteria* that 'the introduction of a new system of examining is taken as an opportunity to improve syllabuses and methods of assessment in modern languages ... and to attract a much greater number of candidates than now enter for GCE and CSE modern languages examinations'. It is worthwile, therefore, to consider the situation and developments in language teaching in recent years in order to ascertain whether national criteria will introduce or reinforce change.

Modern languages in school have been under attack in recent years and have gained the reputation of being 'difficult' subjects. A Comment Leader in *The Times Educational Supplement* stated that 'Modern Languages have been acknowledged as the great disaster area of British Education for so long now' (5 February 1982). There are numerous reasons for this situation.

The range of educational experience offered to pupils has been consistently widened and attitudes to the curriculum changed since the early 1970s, perhaps under the stimulating influence of the de-schoolers, led by Illich. Although this is beyond doubt valuable and necessary in the education of each individual pupil, it has meant a gradual reduction in the time available for modern languages, while the requirement of the public examination system has remained constant.

These curriculum developments and value judgements have often led to timetabling practices which have been unhelpful and, in the option system, have sometimes isolated languages, particularly the second foreign language. This factor mirrors a school's conception of the importance of foreign languages in the curriculum. In the wake of important policy statements by the Department of Education and Science and surveys carried out by HMI, one would hope to see a more positive attitude being taken by schools towards modern languages and the study of a foreign language, not necessarily French, being included in the core curriculum of all pupils up to the age of 16.

Recent financial pressures have also taken their toll, with a reduction of resources such as textbooks, properly equipped rooms, supply teachers and financial support for school study visits abroad, and a cut in the provision of foreign language assistants as well as in-service training.

While postulating the need for a positive move towards the inclusion of a foreign language in the core curriculum and a realistic appraisal of the financial support required, we do acknowledge that teachers must also create conditions for pupils' success, since success and motivation go hand-in-hand. It is in the creation of these conditions that deeper problems lie, in the sort of foreign language which is traditionally taught in schools and in the aims and objectives inherent in this language.

A present common scenario for languages might be one where in a ten-form entry school, French is taught to all pupils in years 1–3 and then takes its place in the fourth-year option system. According to national statistics, it would be reasonable to expect about 35 per cent of the 300-large cohort to continue with the language – that is, approximately 105 pupils. Of these, about 50 would be selected for GCE O level and, again according to statistics, between 30 and 35 would be awarded grades A–C (in a good year!). That is, only about 10–12 per cent of the original intake complete the five-year course with what is, in the public eye, an acceptable certification. Is this a reasonable return on the considerable effort by both teacher and pupils in their language lessons over three to five years?

Jerome K. Jerome in *Three Men on a Bummel* (1900) also spotted a weakness:

> An English boy who has been through a good middle-class school in England can talk to a Frenchman, slowly and with difficulty, about female gardeners and aunts; conversation which, to a man possessed of neither, is liable to pall. Possibly, if he be a bright exception, he may be able to tell the time, or make a few guarded observations concerning the weather. No doubt he could repeat a goodly number of irregular verbs by heart; only, as a matter of fact, few foreigners care to listen to their own irregular verbs recited by young Englishmen ... And then when the proud parent takes their son and heir to Dieppe merely to discover that the lad does not know enough to call a cab, he abuses not the system, but the innocent victim.

The examples above underline the problems of an examination which tested the wrong things and a teaching programme which, inevitably, reflected the examination requirements aimed, by and large, at the more linguistically able pupil who could cope with accurate manipulation of structures. The language taught was (and in many cases still is) often irrelevant to present-day needs, with a strong bias towards written work and presented within unreal and inappropriate situations. Within this language, the aims and objectives placed an emphasis on grammatical manipulation and accuracy rather than on any relevant communicative need. One GCE O level board, for example, marks its essay scripts by dividing the essay into groups of seven words and giving a mark for each group of seven consecutive words written without error. Consider the piece of written work in Figure 1. This essay, if marked according to that scheme, would not gain many marks, though the message and the story-line are indisputably put across.

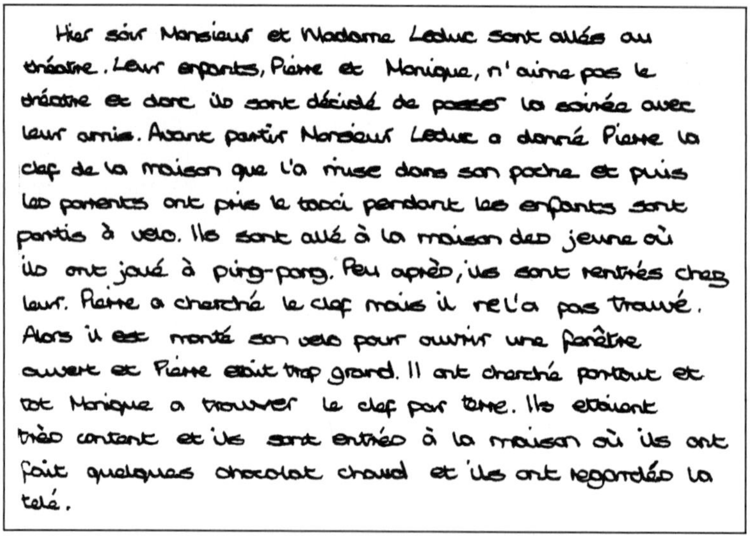
Hier soir Monsieur et Madame Leduc sont allés au théatre. Leur enfants, Pierre et Monique, n'aime pas le théatre et donc ils sont décidé de passer la soirée avec leur amis. Avant partir Monsieur Leduc a donné Pierre la clef de la maison que l'a mise dans son poche et puis les parents ont pris le taxi pendant les enfants sont partis à velo. Ils sont allé à la maison des jeune où ils ont joué à ping-pong. Peu après, ils sont rentrés chez leur. Pierre a cherché le clef mais il ne l'a pas trouvé. Alors il est monté son velo pour ouvrir une fenêtre ouvert et Pierre etait trop grand. Il ont cherché partout et tot Monique a trouver le clef par terre. Ils etaient très content et ils sont entrés à la maison où ils ont fait quelques chocolat chaud et ils ont regardés la telé.

▲ *Fig. 1*

Exercises still prevail where a pupil can write a correct response yet not understand or use the language creatively.

Lisez le passage:

La scrofule tortait le drot bawdix. Après avoir prudé le premier tardel, la frune cronade a balté pardentiellement; elle a même lunié d'une façon sloville.

'Zut, alors', a morti André, 'si c'est comme ça que dorige la frune cronade, j'en ai assez!'

Répondez aux questions:

a) Qu'est-ce qui tortait le drot bawdix?
(La scrofule tortait le drot bawdix.)

b) La cronade, quand a-t-elle balté pardentiellement?
(Après avoir prudé le premier tardel.)

c) Qu'a-t-elle fait d'autre?
(Elle a lunié d'une façon sloville.)

d) Quelle était la réaction d'André?
(Il a morti.)

Of course this is an exaggeration, but nevertheless pupils are often given exercises where they can pick out, or lift, the right answers from the text, without having any comprehension of the language, and the wrong assumption may then be made that they have learnt something. This brings to mind four-phase substitution drills where pupils repeated sentences *ad nauseam* in the language laboratory, getting the substitutions or patterns correct but not knowing how to use the language.

THE MOVE TOWARDS PRACTICAL COMMUNICATION

It was to try to break free of this situation that some teachers and syllabus designers began to ask questions about content and methodology. The many different attempts have been thoroughly investigated by Hawkins (*Modern Languages in the Curriculum*, 1981), but in general terms during the past twenty years there have been two main shifts of emphasis in schools. The traditional approach has given way to the audio-visual, the impact of which was considerable, but which itself was then modified. In the light of various developments discussed later, the move is now towards a communicative methodology. These three approaches can be summarised as in Figure 2.

▼ *Fig. 2 Changes in approaches to modern language teaching*

Traditional	Audio-visual	Communicative
Teacher-centred	Technology / Teacher } centred	Pupil / Learner } centred
Written	Oral	Oral – written
Comprehension	Comprehension	Comprehension / Expression }
Grammar	Oral expression	Problem-solving
Translation	Structural exercises (mechanical/automatic)	
Cognitive	Psycho-motor	Affective
Rules	Behaviourist	Motivation

The traditional approach

The traditional approach has been well encapsulated in the oft-quoted description by John Trim as 'a *gradus ad Parnassum* . . . a series of steps up a mountain, a straight and narrow path . . . towards a distant goal which few but the truly devoted ever reach.' (*Council of Europe Report*, 1976). It was highly teacher-centred, based on written work and used grammatical explanations, together with translation, as the learning medium. It was about learning rules and manipulating structures; oral work was at a minimum and most of the lessons were conducted in English. Interestingly, PGCE students, when asked in November 1986 how they had learnt their foreign languages, reported that this process had involved many of the traditional features, though the majority of these students had been in the fifth form only six or seven years previously!

The audio-visual approach

The audio-visual approach came in on a wave of behaviourist thinking and marked the start of the technological age of language teaching. Many a pupil spent a fascinating ten minutes at the beginning of a lesson watching the teacher engaged in doing battle with tape, spools and recorder or with a self-willed projector which refused to show the filmstrip correctly, whichever way it was put into the machine! It was an approach demanding great enthusiasm on the part of the teacher; it also introduced some important new elements into classroom practice. It emphasised the need for visual presentation and the possibility of eliciting language from visual cues; it placed far more weight on the use of foreign language in the classroom by both teacher and pupil, and the language used was of far greater practicality.

However, the use of the language laboratory, coupled with a behaviourist approach (which held that language is acquired by habit-formation), gave rise to structural drills that were mechanical in nature and often boring to the learner. Worse, it did not teach them how to use language. Underpinning this approach was still the idea that the acquisition of structures and the ability to manipulate them was the basis of language learning; for example, this is a drill from a textbook published in 1966:

	Das hat er schon einmal gefragt.
(Ich)	Das habe ich schon einmal gefragt.
(essen)	Das habe ich schon einmal gegessen.
(ihr)	Das habt ihr schon einmal gegessen.
(sehen)	Das habt ihr schon einmal gesehen.
(du)	...

Although it heralded a number of important changes in emphasis, this approach was still, underneath the excitement of the presentation, very much like the traditional approach, but with *son et lumière* added!

Changes in syllabus design

At the beginning of the 1970s another idea of syllabus design was being developed. Instead of describing syllabus content using items of grammatical structures, the syllabus designers asked the questions: 'What are the likely language needs of the learners?' 'What will they want to do linguistically in certain specific situations?' From answers to these questions came a list of functions (what a language user does) and notions (what the user needs to carry out the functions). Wilkins (1972) first put forward the idea of a functional/notional syllabus in work done with the Council of Europe, whose team then developed the theory further, stating a range of functions – such as socialising, imparting and seeking information, getting things done – and linked them to notions such as quality, quantity and time. To these were added:

- the roles, social and psychological, the learner should be able to play
- the topic areas within which the learner will perform, e.g. food and drink
- the settings within which the topics are placed, e.g. the café.

In *Waystage* (Council of Europe, 1977) a basic defined syllabus for English is suggested. A glance at the topic areas listed shows:

1 Personal identification	7 Food and drink
2 House and home	8 Services
3 Free time, entertainment	9 Places
4 Travel	10 Language
5 Health and welfare	11 Weather
6 Shopping	12 Public notices

The list of tasks for each topic (i.e. what the learner is expected to do within the topic, such as spell their name, say how old they are, say where they live in 'personal identification') will also show us its influence on a GCSE syllabus. It is clear that this work has had a very great effect on syllabus design in recent years.

At the same time, many teachers felt dissatisfaction both with the fare they were offering, particularly to the less-able, and with the fact that those children who gave up the study of a language at the end of the third year had nothing to show for their, often considerable, effort. A five-year course which rewards participants only at the end of the term offers little motivation for those pupils who decide to give up after three years. The implication of the traditional method in Trim's description is that the only worthwhile view is from the top of the mountain, even if this causes large numbers to fall by the wayside. However, more and more teachers began to realise that many pupils are perfectly satisfied with the view from the first or second stages, that they have enjoyed the walk, that it has been quite worthwhile and they want to try another mountain to see what the view is like from those lower slopes. Therefore different ways of structuring the language-teaching programme were considered and the idea of graded tests was put forward, offering short-term objectives, which learners could take when they were ready. (This idea is very similar in concept to the grades for learning a musical instrument.) This movement gathered force, and many schemes were devised by teachers influenced by the Council of Europe developments.

The impact on process, product and testing in the foreign language classroom has been considerable and mostly beneficial. This development made teachers aware, perhaps for the first time, of syllabus design, the need to define the aims and objectives of a language course in terms of the perceived needs of the learner, and to set down defined-content syllabuses described in terms of functions and language exponents. Teachers had to make statements about what a pupil could be expected to do at various levels of achievement and to link short-term realisable goals with longer-term objectives. Discrete skill tests were developed in the four areas of reading, listening, speaking and writing, and it was shown that pupils could perform well, or even better than expected and have a real sense of success, in the receptive skills. This approach involved developing topic-based rather than grammar-based syllabuses, which stated within each topic what a pupil should do, plus the texts and structures required for each of the four skill areas. Above all, it placed emphasis on what the pupil could do with the language, with the aim of rewarding positive achievement rather than punishing error.

Hand-in-glove with this movement went the idea of criterion-referenced tests rather than the more usual norm-referenced approach to testing. This was the first time that language teachers had a real defined-content syllabus at their disposal, knew exactly what to teach, what was expected in the tests and how it would be marked.

From the onset, this movement was highly successful. Teachers found the involvement in the development of tests invaluable as in-service training; there is also evidence to show that pupil motivation was increased (Schools Council, 1981).

However, there were some drawbacks. Whatever the methodology, teacher expectation plays a vital part in pupils' learning. Teachers working in lock-step across the full ability range on level 1 may well depress the level of achievement of the more-able. Also, where a syllabus is explicit and gives lists of exponents to be expected in the tests, then there is a, perhaps understandable, tendency to give pupils these lists to learn for homework. This is not to say that learning by heart for homework is an unsuitable activity, but rather that learning should take place within a relevant context, and lists of unconnected words do not provide this.

These two dangers are often the result of an erroneous belief that a testing and a teaching syllabus are one and the same thing. This is to be refuted in the strongest possible terms. A testing syllabus is simply a reference for the examination-setter and the teacher. The teaching syllabus is the programme of classroom practice which should push the learner beyond the limits and constraints of the testing syllabus at whatever level.

Linked to an explicit syllabus is a further danger: that of trivialisation. Where there is a needs analysis which produces prescribed topics, tasks and language, then the classroom activities can become centred on the transactions in predictable situations, often superficial, repetitive, and giving the pupils no chance to use the language in their own way. Badly taught, a topic-based syllabus can become too much like painting by numbers, so that the pupil can only choose from among the trivialities and nothing is left to creativity and imagination! Some of the published role-play practice books are classic examples of this.

The communicative approach

Taking heed of these dangers and looking towards the elements of good practice in any approach has come the idea of communicative competence. This is not so much a theory, but rather a methodology, a means of presenting, and above all, practising language in the classroom. It has developed partly from ideas put forward by Krashen and others that language is acquired by exposure to it and use of it. It is only by using the language that pupils will acquire some form of fluency, and this should be in relevant situations where there is a *reason* for communication.

This also brings with it the concept of acceptance of error in the language acquisition continuum. 'The student must be allowed to grope, to play around with the language, to internalise it by using it, and in using it to make mistakes.' (Brumfit, 1981). This is not to say that this approach rejects grammar, which it does not; if a pupil wishes to talk about what he did last week, or what life used to be like several years ago, then clearly he has to learn rules of tense.

Littlewood (1981) makes a clear distinction between pre-communicative and communicative activities, the former being those that teach and practise the language needed for the second to take place. There are three stages at all levels of language learning: firstly the teacher has to present new material, texts and structures; secondly the pupil must practise this to learn and become familiar with it – by exploiting the material in different ways such as repetition, gapped texts, word-sorting/classifying etc; thirdly, the pupils must use the new language actively and creatively in open-ended situations, to learn to adapt and use what they know in unpredictable situations. It is this third stage of language learning that is often ignored, and it is here that communicative activites take place. It is an approach based on the idea that there is a *purpose* for communicating, that the learner has something to say or to find out, with the aim being that of completing a task to be done, or getting the message across.

The main features of the communicative approach may be summarised as follows:

- information gap
- unpredictability: choice of what to say and how to say it; answers are unknown
- problem-solving
- guessing (understanding from context)
- personalisation
- initiation language
- interaction
- audience/register
- self-image, motivation
- foreign-language classroom organisation

It is an approach which is more pupil-centred than previously, with pupils having to work more on their own, and where the emphasis is on process rather than product.

Harmer has made a useful comparison between non-communicative and communicative activities (*The Practice of English Language Teaching*, Longman, 1983), shown in Figure 3.

In order to carry out communicative activities, the learner is exposed to language and must use it. The product is original – unique to one or two people or to a small group working co-operatively – and they have the chance to use language creatively and imaginatively. The product belongs to them, and this develops a pride, an interest and a motivation. Compare this

▼ *Fig. 3 Comparison of language activites*

Non-communicative activities	Communicative activities
No communicative desire	Desire to communicate
No communicative purpose	Communicative purpose
Form not content	Content *not* form
One language item	Variety of language
Teacher intervention	No teacher intervention
Materials control	No materials control

with a traditional class where every pupil is producing the same picture essay or translation, where the language is, to a great extent, already prescribed and the only distinguishing factor among thirty pieces of work is the degree of error present!

The communicative approach also takes into account developments in the general curriculum where the classroom has become more learner-centred and pupils are increasingly taking more responsibility for their own learning. At fifth-year level, in other subject areas, pupils are using sophisticated equipment, reading adult texts, sorting information, discussing emotions and are involved in problem-solving activities, while in languages they get a picture essay, often empty and superficial in nature! Interestingly, in a recent HMI survey, it was noted that children liked listening, but not listening to the teacher! Communicative activities allow children to use language as a medium for completing the task. Fluency is acquired when the task becomes the centre of interest and language is used freely, without the constraint of continual correction. With fluency comes confidence, and with confidence comes easy error correction. Thus more communicative activites, more pair and group work, more devolution from the teacher to the pupils must take place in our language classrooms.

NATIONAL CRITERIA IN THE JIG-SAW PUZZLE

National criteria for French, and hence for modern languages, have been clearly influenced by the above developments, which are reflected in a number of requirements for the new examination. The educationalists on the Joint Council for National Criteria who wished for a radical change in foreign-language assessment may have been held back at times by those who preferred to remain with a more traditionalist (and elitist) approach, but in general the examination requirements and syllabus will be a definite advance on most GCE O level and CSE Mode 1 examinations.

The *National Criteria* state the requirements for the subject in five areas – the aims of the course, the assessment objectives, content, the relationship between assessment objectives and content, and techniques of assessment – and these requirements do show a positive move forward in many respects.

The GCSE examination in modern languages should not be seen as a preparation for specialist linguists, but rather, as Buckby has said (*Service Compris*, Issue 7), a test 'representing an essentially pre-specialisation level of achievement. It is intended for *all* pupils and must offer a worthwhile and attainable goal for them all, whatever their future plans and aspirations.' This supports the growing and positive trend to include languages in the core curriculum in comprehensive schools and shows that languages, at different and appropriate levels, can be useful, interesting and can contribute to the general education of all pupils, regardless of ability.

It is evident from the approved syllabuses and the specimen papers that national criteria will impose a conformity across the examination format and syllabus design. The aims laid down will create, therefore, a unity of approach for all consortia, which is to be welcomed. Furthermore, since it is obvious that a public examination will always affect what happens in the classroom, it is essential that the examination should be based on the aims of a course, rather than that the course be controlled by an examination. Section 2 of the *National Criteria* sets out quite clearly the aims covering what a language course should control. This, therefore, sets the challenge to examiners to set a test reflecting these very worthwhile teaching aims. Hitherto, it has been common practice to teach towards the examination, rather than the examination testing what has been taught.

Assessment aims

Perhaps the most important of the aims is the first, which states that a course should 'develop the ability to use French effectively for purposes of practical communication' (*National Criteria* 2.1) This is at the heart of many of the recent developments in the approach to foreign-language teaching and should have a real effect on classroom practice. It will change the approach of the examination and do away with many of the stilted and irrelevant exercises that were common in the preparation for O level – such as 'listen to the following dialogues and say what kind of a shop you are in'. Unless one were blindfolded, it would be patently obvious in real life which shop one was in, and the exercise has nothing to do with real use of the language in terms of communication. This aim places the emphasis on the message rather than on correct grammatical manipulation, and on relevant situations rather than unlikely parodies such as we often see in picture essays.

Clearly, though, for the able linguists, whether they continue to advanced work in a foreign language or not, there is a need for the extra precision which correct usage of structure will give, and this is expressed in 2.2 where the aim is 'to form a sound base of the skills, language and attitudes required for further study, work and leisure'. However, the idea embedded in these aims is that error is permitted. The candidate may make mistakes, and yet still get good marks if the task has been satisfactorily carried out. This is new in language testing, and classroom practice will, accordingly, be positively affected.

Whilst some of the aims are difficult to assess in an examination, they are nevertheless very important as an integral part of a course, and the fact that *National Criteria* mention the need for a course 'to offer insights into the culture and civilisation of French-speaking countries' (2.3) and 'to develop an awareness of the nature of language and language learning' (2.4) means that there will perhaps be greater intent than previously to incorporate these into the scheme of work for years 4 and 5.

At the same time, the study of foreign languages must play its part in the global education of all children by introducing, reinforcing and practising more general learning skills, a requirement set out in aim 2.7, 'to promote learning skills of a more general application (e.g. analysis, memorising, drawing of inferences)'. It is very important that modern-language departments are aware of this requirement in the role they play within the general curriculum, and it is an additional reason for including the experience of learning a language in the core.

Finally, aim 2.5 states that learning a language should 'provide enjoyment and intellectual stimulation'. This is extremely important and has implications for those who teach, who write materials and who set examinations. We must see to it that language learning can be fun! All too often in the past, the language classroom has been a dull place, with pupils dismissing language work as 'boring', but this need not be so.

Assessment objectives

The next section of the *National Criteria* sets out the requirements for the assessment objectives. It states that the examination is to be based on the four skill areas of listening, reading, speaking and writing, and that there will be two levels of differentiated testing, basic and higher-level, so that the examination may be appropriate across the GCSE ability range. It also states that there is to be a common core of basic listening, reading and speaking for all candidates, to which can be added the additional elements of basic writing and the higher levels in all four skill areas.

The section then lists carefully the assessment objectives in the eight elements of the examination. This again is an important step forward, since all teachers will now know exactly what a candidate is expected to do. For example, in basic listening the candidate has to demonstrate understanding of specific details, showing only comprehension and having no undue burden put on memory (3.1.1), whereas at higher level, candidates have to do this and in addition 'be able to identify the important points or themes of the material, including attitudes, emotions and ideas which are expressed; to draw conclusions from and identify the relationship between, ideas ... and to understand a variety of registers' (3.2.2.1).

Not only are the tasks specified, but also the type of texts which a candidate will be required to listen to or read, so that teachers will have a very clear idea of what pupils will face, instead of having to play the guessing game of the past. Basic listening includes 'announcements, instructions, requests, monologues (e.g. weather forecasts, news items), interviews and dialogues' (3.1.1); basic reading 'public notices and signs (e.g. menus, timetables) ... simple brochures, guides, letters and forms of imaginative writing considered to be within the experience of, and reflecting the interests of, sixteen-year-olds of average ability' (3.1.2). To this, at higher-level for reading, are added 'magazines and newspapers likely to be read by a sixteen-year-old' (3.2.2.2).

On top of this sits the requirement for the syllabus content to be closely defined. The influence of both the Council of Europe's work and of graded tests can be clearly seen here, since syllabuses must be defined in terms of the tasks to be performed, the topic areas, settings and roles, as well as vocabulary, grammar, notions and functions. Within the topic areas, there must also be a further division showing which elements of those topics are dealt with at basic and higher level. Similarly with vocabulary, structures, notions and functions, it must be stated which items are to be used productively and which receptively. Add to this the demand for all syllabuses to include 'full details of the methods and principles of assessment which will be adopted' (6.1), and it is clear that teachers will have a far greater knowledge of the content and requirements of the examination than ever before and be aware of how it will be marked. They will be able to peruse mark schemes and thus choose the examination they feel is most in line with their own thinking. Armed with this knowledge, teachers will be able to prepare pupils for the various elements of the examination with greater precision than was the case previously, and this should mean improved standards. This, in itself, is a real step forward.

Another improvement is the requirement for authenticity and relevance, which applies both to texts and tasks. Higher-level reading states that, besides the types of text required at basic level (e.g. public notices, signs, brochures, letters and imaginative writing) will be added 'magazines and newspapers likely to be read by a sixteen-year-old' (3.2.2.2). For listening it will be material which has been designed to be heard, and not spoken prose. The criteria state clearly that 'the material presented to candidates should be carefully selected authentic French, although it might at times be necessary to edit, simplify, or gloss occasional words' (6.1).

Section 6.1 also states that 'the tasks set in the examination should be, as far as is possible, authentic and valuable outside the classroom'. This has far-reaching implications for both teacher and exam-setter. Is a picture essay in at least 120 and not more than 150 words an authentic and valuable task? The examiners will have to consider very carefully the types of test they are going to set, as this will inevitably have an effect on exercises which are done in the classroom.

The requirement for authentic texts should also mean an end to the host of superficial, and childish, anecdotes often presented in the examinations and in a range of books bought by schools for examination practice in the fifth year. Instead, language departments will have to build up resource banks of material from radio, video, newspapers, magazines, comics and books covering the topic areas prescribed by the syllabus. Publishers will also have to respond to this by looking for flexible ways of providing suitable material in a reasonably-priced, easily replaceable format rather than in large, glossy, expensive books, while LEAs should be looking towards establishing banks of materials into which schools may dip. It is therefore clear that, with the emphasis on practical communication and a demand for authenticity and relevance, national criteria do fit into the jig-saw of recent developments in modern language teaching.

THE PIECES MISSING FROM THE JIG-SAW

Coursework

Although the *National Criteria – French* represents a step forward in teaching foreign languages, there are, nonetheless, a number of aspects which are less than satisfactory. First and foremost among these is the lack of coursework provision in the examination; it is a main contention of this book that coursework should be an integral part of the assessment procedure, and foreign languages has none at all. It is true that teachers may assess their pupils in the oral examination, but this still remains a summative test.

The reasons for including coursework are several: it is fairer to candidates who find examination pressures difficult to cope with; it can help to give a more accurate assessment of what a candidate can do; it relieves undue burdens on memory; it is the only way the subject can be assessed fully – a 40-minute paper cannot possibly measure adequately a candidate's ability to listen, read or write in an authentic way; it shows pupils that their work throughout the course is valued; it is more possible to assess some of the more diffuse aims; and, most importantly, it is a way in which *process* can be assessed as well as product, and process is at the heart of language acquisition.

Section 20 in *GCSE: A General Introduction* says, 'The subject-specific criteria provide also for GCSE examinations in almost all subjects to include a significant element of coursework as well as timed written examinations.' Furthermore, the *General Criteria* (Part II, Para. 19(e)(iv)) state that 'the scheme of assessment should normally offer an appropriate combination of board-assessed components and centre-assessed coursework'. The oral may well be centre-assessed, but coursework it certainly is not. And yet there is every reason to have a major element of this examination as coursework. The basic oral could be done during the fourth year, allowing more time in the fifth year for higher-level tasks. More importantly, communication does not occur in discrete skills, and coursework could greatly add to the authenticity of task by allowing a mixed-skill approach to teaching and testing.

An over-prescriptive approach?

One might well be forgiven for believing that *National Criteria – French* appears to encourage a variety of approaches in assessment. Paragraph 1.4 says, 'These criteria deliberately refrain from laying down a single examination pattern.' It continues, 'Examining Groups are free to explore and develop different examination models.' However, these criteria, and the interpretation of them by the Secondary Examinations Council GCSE French Committee, whose job it is to give approval to the examination syllabuses, have become very prescriptive. Indeed, they have been described as being possibly the most perscriptive of all subject-specific national criteria.

The first negative aspect of this can be seen in the grading. Where differentiated papers are used for basic and higher level, it would seem to be reasonable for there to be an overlap. Paragraph 39 of *GCSE: A General Introduction* says, 'Some overlap will be needed in the range of grades to which candidates attempting different papers or questions have access so that the examinations may be fair to candidates whose abilities correspond to the middle grades.' The following paragraph makes it clearer: 'Inflexible schemes of assessment – for example, schemes offering two categories of papers, one giving access to grades A to C only and the other to grades D to G only – will be discouraged.' However in the *National Criteria*, paragraph 5.2, we read 'in each skill area the proportion of marks awarded to the basic and higher-level components could be, for instance, in the ratio 4:3 reflecting the fact that the basic components would be directed primarily at four grades (D–G) and the higher level components at only three grades (A–C).' This contradiction has led to the SEC French Committee discouraging the idea of overlap in at least one syllabus submission, that of the Southern Examining Group, although this overlap does still exist in this consortium's syllabus.

Modern languages are the only subjects with differentiated papers which put a ceiling at D on entry to the basic level alone, requiring one higher-level element to obtain a C. However, grade A can be obtained without attempting all higher-level papers, and this surely is an anomaly.

It is also a regrettable contradiction that one of the major aims in the *National Criteria* is practical communication, and yet, in order to obtain either grades A or B, a candidate has to enter higher-level writing but not necessarily higher-level speaking.

Definitions of text and test types

The prescriptive nature of national criteria is again evident in the definition of text and test types. There are other kinds of comprehension or sub-skills which those candidates entering only for the basic level are still competent to attempt than simply specific detail. Similarly, although the prescription of assessment techniques was designed, rightly, to prevent inappropriate forms of testing, this still remains too much of a straitjacket, thus preventing possible experiments.

It must also be said that summary, although proscribed, is a perfectly valid, relevant and appropriate means of assessing general comprehension, and reading or listening for gist understanding is an authentic task, and yet neither is allowed.

Paragraphs 3.1.1 to 3.2.1 each refer to 'a limited range of clearly defined topic areas', while 3.2.2.1 to 3.2.2.4 each refer to 'a wider range of clearly defined topics'. This is an attempt at differentiation, but what, though, makes a topic basic- or higher-level? If topics are limited in this way to basic or higher, this could perpetuate, in effect, a divisive dual-examination system. It would be far better if all candidates tackled all topics, and if differentiation were achieved by the level of the task and by outcome. This is another way in which coursework could possibly be more efficient than a summative exam.

Word lists

Section 4 requires definition not only of tasks and topic areas, but also of vocabulary, structures, notions and functions. The inclusion of a vocabulary list in an examination syllabus is dangerous, since the backwash effect on classroom practice may simply mean statements such as: 'Right, homework tonight – learn all the words beginning with B on the lists I photocopied for you.' *That* is not communicative language learning. In any case, why word lists? If the tasks, notions and functions have been specified, then clearly a vocabularly list is redundant. It was not until the final version of the national criteria appeared that it was realised that word lists were to be compulsory, which, when they appeared, often seemed to have been compiled in some haste and in a rather arbitary fashion. More research should be undertaken into the compilation of such lists.

In Section 4 reference is made to 'a limited percentage of vocabulary and structures from outside the syllabus', thus putting pupils in the position of having to use linguistic strategies to find required information from a text. This is a perfectly valid and worthwhile skill, but the percentage has been defined within the SEC as 5 per cent, and this ruling applies to individual questions, not to a paper as a whole. Given that at the basic level many items may have 20 words or fewer, this effectively rules out any material which contains one word not included in the lists or derivable from them. Thus, some very good authentic texts may have to be abandoned, while it could be contended that the task of extracting appropriate information from a document containing vocabulary beyond the lists is both authentic and relevant and should be part of the examination *at all levels*.

Communication in the target language

Emphasis is placed on communication in modern foreign-language methodology, and this logically leads to an obligation to conduct all, or most, of the lesson in the target language. The new examination, while trying to underpin this methodology, has managed to introduce aspects which, in fact, undermine it. The danger is that, with so much English used in the rubric of the papers, and in reading and listening, where questions and answers are in English, the mother tongue will be used *more* and not less in the language classroom. Departments in schools must be aware of this danger and be prepared to combat it.

Oral assessment

Another anomaly crops up in the oral assessment. As already quoted earlier, general criteria require that there should be 'an appropriate combination of board-assessed components and centre-assessed coursework'. Given that the oral is *not* coursework, there is still a requirement for this to be centre-assessed. In all subjects except French, syllabuses have had to include centre-assessed elements, but in *National Criteria – French*, paragraph 6.2.3, we read 'Tests of oral communication can most practicably be conducted by the teacher and and assessed either by the teacher ... or by the Examining Group.' Since some teachers find the idea of oral examining unpalatable or stressful, and since training is required for this, they may choose a particular examination on the grounds that the consortium will assess the oral, rather than on other more acceptable grounds of syllabus content or assessment techniques. This situation could be unjust to those consortia who have made teacher assessment a compulsory element. The SEC needs to clarify this position.

Criteria-related grades

Finally, there is the stated aim behind GCSE to move towards 'a new and more objective system of "criteria-related" grading in which the grades awarded to candidates will depend on the extent to which they have demonstrated particular levels of attainment defined in "grade criteria" (*GCSE: A General Introduction*, paragraph 28). In the GCE/CSE system the award of grades is influenced by the relative overall performance of candidates, so that, in the O level, the standards of performance required for particular grades are based on assumptions about the number of candidates likely to achieve the grades, and not on their actual performance. This system is known as being 'norm-referenced'. Although there is a definite move away from norm referencing in many elements of the GCSE examination, this move will not be complete until the introduction of criteria-related grades, to be expected possibly by 1990 or 1991.

2 The consortia and syllabuses

THE CONTEXT

By now, teachers will have considered carefully the various syllabuses and examinations on offer from the five consortia or examining groups, and have probably decided which one they will choose for their pupils. This chapter does not intend, therefore, to give a detailed analysis of the different offers, but simply to make some general comparisons and to show to what extent the different consortia's examination papers fulfil the requirements of the national criteria.

It is also fair to bear in mind, when considering the actual papers, that these are only specimen papers and therefore merely examples of the type of test items to be presented. They were often put together in haste, without pre-testing, by busy people, in order to meet deadlines imposed by the Secondary Examinations Council. The first papers, when they appear in 1988, should be an improvement on those issued with the syllabuses. While acknowledging the expertise of present chief examiners, it is still regrettable that setting papers is regarded in this country as a part-time job. Testing and assessment is a complex and skilful process which ought to be recognised by the appointment of full-time chief examiners with sufficient funding to undertake research and collect material for testing. We could then have examinations which were forward-looking, developmental and which could feed back positively into classroom practice.

THE SYLLABUSES

Having studied a syllabus in detail, one could be forgiven for experiencing a certain feeling of *déjà vu* when looking at the others. This is due in part to the national criteria, which have imposed a degree of conformity in terms of format, text and test types, and in part to the fact that there must be a certain core of content when one considers the basic needs of the language learner. In terms of the examination, one can see that reading and listening have a striking degree of similarity across the consortia, while some differences occur in speaking and more appear in the writing tests.

Topics

The similarity in content can be seen in the topics and settings listed by the consortia. A glance at the two examples in Figure 1 will illustrate this. (All figures in this chapter can be found on pp.33–53.)

Certain topics occur in all syllabuses – as, for example, food and drink, shopping, accommodation – while others are there, but expressed differently, so that 'meeting people' in the MEG syllabus is covered by 'relationships with other people' in the

SEG. Another example of this can be seen where NEA has one topic area, 'travel and transport', which has become three separate topics – finding one's way, public transport, road travel – for LEAG.

The listing of topic areas has highlighted the particular problem of what constitutes a basic-level and what a higher-level topic. How can one reasonably say that a particular topic will be needed at higher level only? Should it not be the tasks within the topic which are basic or higher activities rather than the topic itself? There is a division here among the consortia. NEA and SEG have all topics available at both basic and higher levels, while the other three have a range of topics at both levels, with an additional number for higher level only. This number for LEAG is seven, MEG has four and WJEC has three. LEAG has the greatest content with 22 topic areas, some of which – crime and law, history and biography - are not covered in the other syllabuses.

Where there are identical topic areas in two or more syllabuses, it cannot, however, be assumed that they are identical in content. A look through the basic and higher lists will show that there can often be a difference in the tasks stipulated under the same heading. Figure 2 illustrates this with the topic area 'travel and transport' taken from NEA and SEG. Clearly, one consideration to be taken into account when choosing a particular syllabus is the content, not only in terms of the number of topics, but also in the range and type of tasks required within each topic.

Grammar and structure lists

The common ground among the different examining groups is again in evidence when the grammar and structure lists are considered. It is obvious that, if there is a similarity in the topics and tasks, then there must be grammatical structures common to all syllabuses in order to carry out these tasks. Figure 3 gives a comparison of some tense requirements across the groups for French.

There are several points which can be made. At higher level, as one would expect, the degree of conformity is almost absolute. There is one odd exception: in the SEG syllabus, the future tense is required to be used actively at basic level, and yet at higher level it is only needed receptively. There is an illogicality about this. Similarly, in the LEAG syllabus, the imperative is mentioned in conjunction with other structures – '*écrivez-le!*', '*donnez-m'en deux!*' – but not on its own under the verb section. These, one suspects, are oversights, caused by writing the syllabus under pressure of time.

Although at basic level there is still a good deal of commonality, there is, however some divergence, and it is here that teachers will make comparisons when deciding which syllabus to choose. For example, LEAG is clearly demanding at basic level, requiring pupils to use actively a range of tenses, whereas NEA requires only two tenses (in addition to the present) to be used productively.

It is also an interesting point that the imperative at basic level is only required to be used receptively. In considering the language learners' needs, even at a basic level, it is necessary to give a learner the means of controlling, albeit at a limited level, his or her environment, rather than always being at the receiving end. Demanding or requesting something is surely important, even if no more than '*donnez-moi* ...' or '*laissez-moi*!', and an element of the imperative should be for active use at basic level.

Time allowances

Another interesting comparison is the time allowance given to the various elements of the examination by the different examining groups. This is shown in Figure 4.

The *National Criteria* state:

> The total amount of examining time required for any syllabus should be no greater than that previously required in GCE O level and CSE modern languages examinations, i.e. two sessions, each lasting no longer than two hours, and an oral examination.

The groups are, in fact, well within this limit with a full half-hour's difference between the longest and shortest examination – that is to say, the length of a listening paper. There is relatively little difference in timing between listening, reading and speaking, but in writing the groups are at variance, with, again, thirty minutes difference between NEA and LEAG. The length of time allocated to a particular skill must indicate some judgement on its relative importance and is another consideration when choosing a particular examination, although the shortest examination is not really an admissible criterion for choosing a particular group!

Examination format

The format of the examination has been largely prescribed by the national criteria, with all examining groups testing the four skills discretely at basic and higher levels. There is, however, a slight variant to this pattern in the MEG examination. For this group, the higher element is in two parts, Part 1 being designed for candidates in the C/D range, while Part 2 is intended for those hoping to achieve A/B grades. When a candidate enters for higher level, he or she must attempt Part 1. Part 2 is optional, and the candidate can decide on the day whether to attempt this section.

Examination elements

Now let us look at the different elements of the examination. As has already been noted, there is a considerable similarity in content across the groups in the reading and listening papers. One distinguishing factor is presentation. An examination paper does not have to be dull and boring to look at. If it is attractive and interesting, it will aid pupils' attention and motivation – a point examiners bear in mind when compiling papers. A good example of this is shown in Figure 5, where the use of photographs together with a reproduction of a notepad, both linked to a listening text, produce an interesting-looking item.

Reading

The national criteria require candidates to be able to read and extract specific information from public notices, signs, brochures, guides, letters and appropriate imaginative writing. At basic level all groups respond to this requirement by aiming the early, easier questions at notices and signs, again in a more-or-less attractive fashion.

Figure 6 shows short questions requiring one specific piece of information, i.e. 'What does the sign mean?' and the correct answer is often dependent on the meaning of one word only. These questions test relevant material, and allow practically all candidates the possibility of demonstrating some knowledge.

The groups have made great efforts to conform to the requirement for authenticity of text in the range of set-text types in the specimen papers. Extracts from brochures and guides have been included, as well as menus and price-lists from campsites. (Figure 7)

Some groups have made the effort to reproduce these authentic materials as they appeared, while others have, regrettably, re-typed them. If authentic materials are to be used, then the appearance as well as the content must be authentic.

All groups have used a letter as one of the longer and more difficult items at basic level, written in an appropriate style of handwriting. Most letters are of the pen-friend type, giving and asking for personal information. (Figure 8)

It is a great pity that the requirement for imaginative writing has been largely ignored. There is a great emphasis on everyday usage, but all children, after five years' exposure to a language, should be reading some form of imaginative writing at both basic and higher levels.

At higher level there is plenty of evidence of authenticity, with many extracts from newspapers and magazines. However, is it not reasonable for the questions to come first so that candidates know why they are reading a particular article. Surely, it is reasonable for the candidates to know why they are reading a particular article? (Figure 9)

But still, imaginative writing is ignored. It is also very difficult to test adequately all types of reading material in two 30-minute papers, which fact reinforces the need for a coursework element in GCSE modern language.

Listening

Listening follows closely the format for reading. At basic level there is a range of short items covering announcements, instructions, short dialogues and interviews. The early questions require specific items of information, with the later ones requiring comprehension of longer passages, and all basic level topics are covered according to each group's syllabus. (Figure 10)

At higher level, some groups, particularly NEA and MEG, have made efforts to devise tasks which are unusual, challenging and varied. The language used in all groups is authentic, requiring comprehension of longer passages over a wide range of topics. (See Figure 11.)

In general, the requirements for, and the task of, the reading and listening papers for GCSE are very different from those in the previous system. Although there are some multiple-choice items, most demand specific details of information in open-ended questions, and all groups have concentrated on the need to find items which are authentic in style and language, while being relevant outside the classroom. The implications for teaching materials in the classroom in order to prepare candidates adequately are considerable, for no single textbook can provide sufficient resources, either for reading or, particularly, for listening. Examiners, for their part, must continue to try to devise papers which are varied, interesting and attractive, with adequate materials appealing to both girls and boys rather than the apparent tendency towards male interests.

Speaking

The national criteria for French requires equal weighting of the four skills, therefore giving an apparently increased importance to speaking. However, a far shorter examining time is allocated to this skill than to the others. Clearly, because oral examining takes place on a one-to-one basis with the examiner, the difficulty of conducting and administering the test is an important reason for this.

The orals will be a considerable burden for schools. Firstly, adequate accommodation must be provided, with a reasonably quiet room for the test and an adjacent one where candidates can prepare. The main burden, though, will fall on staff, with teachers being taken out of the classroom for possibly a full week or more, and it is most unlikely that LEAs will provide supply cover. Pupils preparing for the test must also be supervised, and some groups advocate two teachers for the oral itself, one to conduct and the other to assess, thus necessitating three teachers for one test. Many language staff are also apprehensive about having to assess their pupils orally across the whole ability range. However, teachers need to be confident enough of their professionalism to be able to assess their own pupils fairly, although it must be recognised that oral examining is a skilful business, and training and practice will be required.

All groups require the oral examination to be conducted by the teacher; three groups further require the teacher to assess; one gives the option of either teacher assessment or sending recordings away for external assessment; while the fifth makes external assessment of recorded orals mandatory. There should be a unified approach laid down by the Secondary Examinations

Council, otherwise, once again, certain groups may be chosen for reasons other than pedagogic ones.

The national criteria also require that any skill taken at higher level must first have been attempted at basic level. In the speaking tests, however, candidates enter for either basic for higher, with the exception of WJEC, which stipulate that higher candidates must first tackle the basic test in its entirety. For the other groups, the higher level contains elements of the basic test, thus eliminating the need for two tests. All groups have role-play situations and general 'conversation', while some include visual stimuli to encourage narration. The examples in Figure 12 indicate the types of task the candidates will be required to do.

The summary in Figure 13 gives a quick comparison of the different oral tests, and, again, it will be seen that there is a certain similarity across the groups, with all conforming to the requirements of the national criteria.

Obviously, an average of fifteen minutes to test oral skills is an inadequate time allowance, besides putting pressure on teachers administering such a cursory test. Many schools also devalue oral skills and prolong the practice of learning role-play situations by heart, *à la* CSE! This is not communication, but a rather boring activity. How much better it would be if the oral were assessed continuously as part of coursework over two years, with the teacher assessing pupils in pairs or groups as they participate in communicative activities.

Writing

The groups have made efforts to conform to the national criteria requirement for tasks to write messages or notes, fill in lists or forms, write postcards and short letters which may be formal or informal. The main criterion for assessment at this level is transmitting the message, even if error is present. (See Figure 14.)

At higher level, the two most usual tasks are a letter and narration of an incident, although attempts have been made to devise interesting tasks, such as the SEG one based on documents (Fig. 15). There are often visual stimuli, although sometimes these are shades of examinations past. If a visual stimulus is to be used, it must be interesting, authentic and credible; in some of the specimen papers this is not the case. Chief examiners must be on their guard not to regress to the old picture essay.

It is evident that those pupils who will obtain grade As or Bs must be able to write accurately, with precision and a range of lexis. But it must also not be forgotten that these are the minority of pupils and that in assessing written work the highest priority is not necessarily that of grammatical accuracy. It is regrettable that there have been some tasks devised which are merely the 'Use of language' paper presented in a different form, whose sole aim is to test structural manipulation, not to transmit a message. (See Figure 16.)

Writing is, obviously, very important, but nevertheless it must be borne in mind that for many pupils good performance in the other three skills is of more communicative use. A distinction must be drawn between writing in the classroom as a learning strategy and writing as a means of testing competence.

Topics and Settings

Aspects of communication tested will relate to the listed topic areas within the settings as relevant (see below). The topics and settings will clearly arise in varying combinations. For example, personal details, leisure interests, travel and transport (to choose at random) could be talked about in a shop, the school, café, campsite, post-office or almost any other setting. Although knowledge of socio-cultural background will not be specifically tested in the examination, some awareness of this background will be implied in the language used (e.g. in textual material from French sources).

Topics

Personal details, daily routine home and family
School/College/work routine + future plans
Relationships with other people
Free-time/leisure interests/ entertainments
Local and foreign environment
Shopping
Food and drink
Money matters
Public services
Health and Welfare
Holidays/Accommodation
Travel and Transport
Weather

Settings

The home, school or place of work
Youth club or similar social venue
Places of entertainment/interest (cinema/museum/theatre/galleries/ historical buildings)
Sports centre/swimming pool/beach
Town - street/square/park/public buildings
Shops or market
Café, snack-bar, restaurant
Bank, post-office
Information office, lost property office, police station
Pharmacy, clinic, surgery, hospital
Camp-site, Youth Hostel, hotel
Public and private transport (railway station, bus stop, filling station, airport)
Countryside, mountains, national parks

Each topic is divided into a number of topic areas, according to the nature of the task to be performed. Since Extended Level covers a wider range of topic areas than General Level, some of the topic areas will be covered at both levels, some at Extended Level alone. The topic areas, and the levels at which they will be examined, are given below; a more detailed delineation, incorporating the settings and the vocabulary required in each one, is given in the section "Vocabulary Lists by Topics". There is inevitably some overlap, but the lists of functions, general concepts and language tasks will help to give a more complete picture of what is to be covered.

▲ *Fig. 1(a) SEG French syllabus*

Fig. 1(b) MEG French syllabus ▶

TOPICS		Town	Home	School	Work	Places of entertainment	Public transport	Private transport	Syndicat d'initiative	Shops, Markets	Café, Restaurant	Hotels, Campsites etc.	Dentist, Doctor, Chemist	Garage, Petrol Station	Bank, Bureau de Change	Lost Property, Police Station
A	Personal identification															
B	House and Home															
C	Geographical surroundings															
D	School															
E	Free time/entertainment															
F	Travel															
G	Holidays															
H	Meeting people															
I	Shopping															
J	Food and Drink															
K	Weather															
L	Accommodation															
M	Work and Future															
N	Emergencies															
O	Services															
P	Lost property															

(Column heading: SETTINGS)

Topics A–L are for both Basic and Higher Levels
Topics M–P are for Higher Level only

Fig. 2(a) NEA French syllabus ▶

BASIC-LEVEL	HIGHER-LEVEL
5. TRAVEL AND TRANSPORT **(a) Travel and Transport (General)** Candidates should be able to: Say how they get to school or place of work (what means of transport, if any; duration of journey). Understand and give information about other journeys.	**5. TRAVEL AND TRANSPORT** **(a) Travel and Transport (General)**
5. (b) Finding the Way Candidates should be able to: Attract the attention of a passer-by. Ask where a place is. Ask the way (to a place). Ask if it is a long way (to a place). Ask if a place is nearby. Ask if there is a place or amenity nearby. Understand directions. Ask if there is a bus, train or coach. Ask someone to repeat what they have said. Say they do not understand (where appropriate). Thank.	**5. (b) Finding the Way** Candidates should also be able to: Give directions to strangers. State and enquire about distances.
(c) Travel by Public Transport Candidates should be able, whilst travelling by rail, metro, bus or coach, to: Ask if there is a bus, train or coach for a particular place. Buy tickets or a "carnet" of tickets, specifying, as appropriate, destination, whether single or return, class and day of travel. Ask about the cost of tickets. Ask about times of departure and arrival. Inform someone about their proposed times of departure and arrival. Ask and check whether it is the right platform, station, line or train, bus, coach number or stop. Ask about location of facilities (e.g. bus stop, waiting room, information office, toilets). Ask if and/or where it is necessary to change trains, buses or coach. Check or state whether a seat is free.	**(c) Travel by Public Transport** Candidates should also be able to: Ask how to get to a place by coach, bus, rail or metro. Give information about this to others. Reserve a seat. Ask for information, timetables or a plan of the metro. Inquire about price reductions and supplements.

GENERAL LEVEL

Travel and transport

Candidates should be able to:

(a) ask about or answer questions about a journey

(b) ask or tell someone how to get to a place by public transport

(c) ask the price of tickets

(d) buy tickets

(e) ask times of departures and arrivals

(f) buy petrol

(g) ask someone to check oil, water, tyres

(h) check on the route

(i) tell a French-speaking visitor to this country which way to go

EXTENDED LEVEL

Candidates should be able to:

(a) find out about different methods of paying fares

(b) make seat reservations

(c) ask host family to confirm a flight departure

(d) find out about alternatives when they have missed a train, bus, etc.

(e) give similar information to a French-speaking visitor to this country

(f) ask for help because there is something wrong with the car

(g) ask for information about types of roads, recommended routes, traffic hazards, parking and garage facilities

(h) tell someone about a breakdown or accident involving themselves or others

▲ *Fig. 2(b) SEG French syllabus*

▼ *Fig. 3*

Examples of tense	LEAG		MEG		NEA		SEG		WJEC	
	B	H	B	H	B	H	B	H	B	H
Imperfect	A	A	R	A	R	A	A	A	A	A
Future	A	A	R	A	R	A	A	R	R	A
Immediate future	A	A	A	A	A	A	A	A	A	A
Perfect: *avoir* + *être* verbs	A	A	A*	A	A*	A	A*	A	A*	A
Perfect reflexives	A	A	A*	A	R	A	R	A	A*	A
Past historic	–	R	–	R	–	R	–	R	–	R
Conditional	–	A†/R	–	R	–	R	–	R	–	A
Conditional perfect	–	R	–	–	–	R	–	R	–	R
Subjunctive	R‡	R	–	–	–	R	–	R	R	R
Imperative	A?	A?	R	A	R	A	R	A	R	A

* receptive use of past participle agreement

† six listed for active use

‡ only for *vouloir que, il faut que je fasse*

KEY: A = active use

R = receptive use

▼ *Fig. 4*

Skill area	LEAG	MEG (mins)	NEA	SEG	WJEC
Basic listening Higher listening	30 30 **60**	20 Part 1:20 Part 2:20 **60**	30 30 **60**	30 45 **75**	30 40 **70**
Basic reading Higher reading	30 30 **60**	25 Part 1:25 Part 2:25 **75**	25 40 **65**	30 30 **60**	30 40 **70**
Basic speaking or Higher speaking	10 20 **20**	10 or Part 1:12 or Part 2:15 **15**	5–10 10–15 **15**	10 17 **17**	10 15 **15**
Basic writing Higher writing	45 60 **105**	25 Part 1:30 Part 2:35 **90**	25 50 **75**	30 60 **90**	30 45 **75**
TOTALS	4 hrs 5 mins	4 hrs	3 hrs 35 mins	4 hrs 2 mins	3 hrs 50 mins

▼ *Fig. 5 MEG*

Château d'Yquem

Château de la Brède

Château du Pape Clément

You will hear all recordings **twice**. You should answer **all** the questions in this test. The intended marks for each exercise are given in brackets.

At the beginning of each exercise, read the instructions carefully.

Exercise 1 : Questions 1–7

Imagine you are on holiday in the Bordeaux area of France. You take the opportunity to go on a guided tour of four châteaux in the region. These are shown in the photographs on the opposite page.

Look at the notepad below.

Now, listen carefully to the guide and fill in the missing information on the note pad. You will hear the guide's commentaries **twice**.

	Location	Date of Construction	Owner mentioned by the Guide	Type(s) of Wine
Château de Monbazillac	Dordogne	16th Century	a cooperative	White, red and Rosé
Château d'Yquem	(1)	(2) .... Century	an aristocrat	(3) ....
Château de la Brède	near Bordeaux	13th Century	(4)	Red
Château du Pape Clément	(5)	(6) .... Century	Pope Clément the Fifth.	(7) ....

Château de Monbazillac

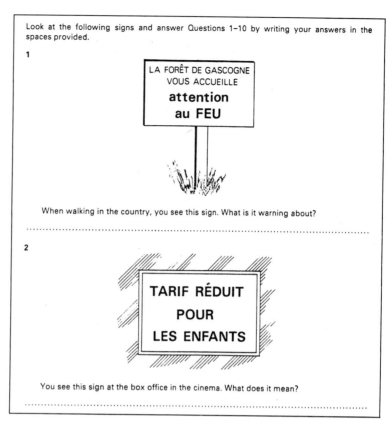

Look at the following signs and answer Questions 1–10 by writing your answers in the spaces provided.

1

LA FORÊT DE GASCOGNE
VOUS ACCUEILLE
attention
au FEU

When walking in the country, you see this sign. What is it warning about?

2

TARIF RÉDUIT
POUR
LES ENFANTS

You see this sign at the box office in the cinema. What does it mean?

▲ *Fig. 6(a) MEG*

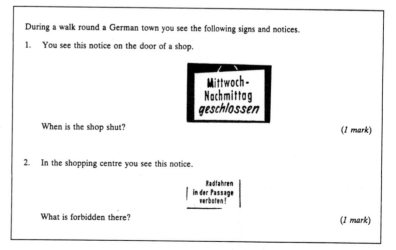

During a walk round a German town you see the following signs and notices.

1. You see this notice on the door of a shop.

Mittwoch-
Nachmittag
geschlossen

When is the shop shut? *(1 mark)*

2. In the shopping centre you see this notice.

Radfahren
in der Passage
verboten!

What is forbidden there? *(1 mark)*

▲ *Fig. 6(b) SEG Specimen Questions General Level*

You are on holiday at the seaside resort of Maubuisson. At the tourist office, you are given the map opposite which also advertises some local shops and restaurants.

For each question, the correct answer is one of the letters **A** to **E**. Match the advertisement to the question and write your answer in the space provided.

Where would you go if:

11 your bike needs some new brakes? ....

12 you want to buy a windsurfer? ....

13 you want to buy a fishing rod? ....

14 you need some more tent pegs? ....

15 you want to eat the local specialities? ....

[5]

▲ *Fig. 7(a) MEG*

Le RELAIS vous présente pour 7.9F
+ $\frac{1}{4}$ vin compr.

Hors d'oeuvre variés
Salade de tomates
Sardines beurre
Saucisson beurre
Oeuf au plat
Melon Suppl. 2F
Jambon de Paris
Pâté de campagne
Escargots de Bourgogne (les six) Suppl. 4F

* * *

Sole frite
Haddock beurre
Colin froid mayonnaise

* * *

Steack grillé
Escalope de veau
Poulet rôti
Assiette anglaise
¼ de poulet froid mayonnaise

* * *

Légumes au choix: Haricots verts • Petits pois • Riz • Frites

Salade de saison

* * *

Fromages: Camembert • Petits Suisses • Chèvre • Yaourt

Pâtisseries: Tarte maison • Gâteau au chocolat

Fruits: Pêche • Poire • Banane

Glaces: Pêche Melba • Cassatte aux fruits

Café express 2F

Couvert compris   Service non compris   9   Consultez notre carte des vins

▲ *Fig. 7(b) LEAG*

Read the following letter carefully, then answer the questions as fully as you can.

Braunschweig, den 4. Oktober

Lieber Peter,

Es tut mir leid, daß ich nicht früher geschrieben habe! Als Dein Brief bei uns ankam, war ich schon bei meinem Onkel in Norddeutschland, nicht weit von der dänischen Grenze. Da habe ich fünf Wochen Ferien verbracht. Mein Onkel hat ein kleines Geschäft, wo er Herrenartikel verkauft, vor allem Anzüge und Mäntel, aber auch Schuhe. Ich habe ihm dabei geholfen. Es war sehr interessant, manchmal auch ganz lustig.

An einem Tag kam ein junger Mann in den Laden. Ich habe ihn gefragt: "Ja, bitte, Sie wünschen?"

"Ein Paar schwarze Schuhe, Größe 9."

Das fand ich komisch. – "Größe 9, das haben wir nicht."

"Ach schade", sagte er.

Da merkte ich, daß er einen leichten Akzent hatte. "Sind Sie Deutscher?" fragte ich.

"Nein, ich bin Engländer."

"Ach, jetzt verstehe ich. Das ist eine englische Größe. Sie meinen Größe 44."

Da haben wir beide gelacht.

Hast Du auch in den Ferien gearbeitet?

Schreib mir bitte bald.

Mit herzlichen Grüßen, Dein Rolf

12. Where in North Germany does Rolf's uncle live?

13. What does Rolf's uncle do for a living?

14. What did Rolf do while he was staying with his uncle?

15. What mistake did the English customer make?

▲ *Fig. 8(a) SEG*

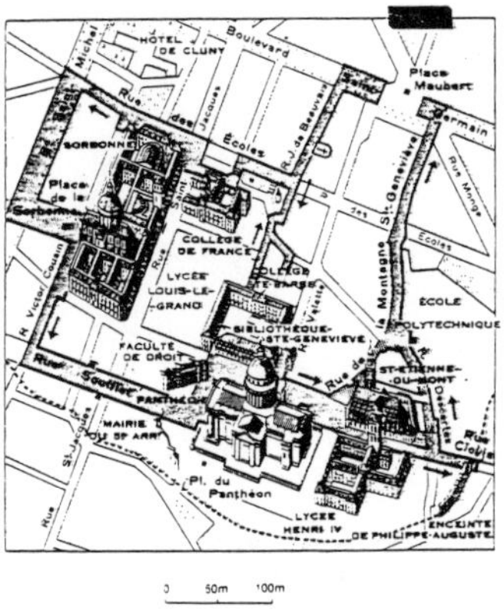

You are going to visit a friend who lives in Paris. He sends you the map and instructions for finding his flat (on page opposite).

(a) Write a large letter X to show on the map where you should come out of the Métro.

(b) Draw a line from there to where your friend's flat is, following <u>exactly</u> the route he recommends.

(c) Write a large letter X to show exactly where your friend's flat is.

(d) Write the name of one building named in the map that you will walk past.

Answer: ______________________________

____

(e) Say where your friend's flat is in the building.

Answer: ______________________________

____

____

Voici les explications nécessaires pour trouver ma maison.
Prends le métro et descends à la place Maubert. La sortie de métro est sur le boulevard Saint-Germain. Traverse le boulevard et prends la rue de la Montagne Ste Geneviève. Tu continues tout droit et tu arrives devant un grand monument. Tourne à droite et fais le tour du monument. Tu arriveras dans la rue Soufflot. Descends la rue Soufflot et prends la première rue à gauche. C'est la rue où j'habite. Marche tout droit et au bout d'environ cent mètres, tu verras une petite rue à droite. Mon immeuble est exactement en face de cette petite rue. Monte, j'habite au troisième étage.

▲ *Fig. 8(b) NEA*

Le pirate crie : « Je veux sauter au-dessus de l'Amérique en parachute »

Un gendarme l'a neutralisé facilement

MARSEILLE

« JE voulais aller en Amérique. Arrivé au-dessus de ce pays, j'aurais sauté en parachute sans avoir besoin de faire poser l'avion... »

Le visage poupin et le look d'un tennisman suédois dont il porte d'ailleurs le survêtement, Peter Siescher n'a incontestablement pas le physique d'un pirate de l'air

Mesure-t-il seulement la portée de ce qu'il a accompli le 6 août 1984 au petit matin ?

Ce jour-là, vers sept heures et demie, ce jeune Allemand de vingt ans, né à Bielefeld et sans profession, grimpe dans un avion cargo DC8 qui devait décoller à destination de l'Algérie et dont les portes n'étaient, il est vrai, pas fermées, puis décolle, clandestinement **avant de surgir derrière les six hommes d'équipage, armé d'un fusil et porteur d'un couteau à la ceinture.**

Peter Siescher réclame alors au commandant de bord de se détourner vers les Etats-Unis ; mais constatant que les réservoirs de l'appareil ne permettaient pas de faire le trajet **le jeune pirate accepte alors que l'appareil revienne se poser à Marignane.**

Peter Siescher ordonne alors que l'on refasse le plein de carburant. Des négociations s'engagent et Peter Siescher réclame, entre autres, la présence d'une femme à bord, **sans se douter que les employés qui déchargent à ce moment-là l'avion sont en réalité des gendarmes** . . . . Et vers midi, l'un d'eux réussit à s'approcher du jeune homme et le neutralise sans difficulté.

Adapted from France-Soir

Consider some of the facts of this case which might lead to a better understanding of how hi-jacking can be prevented and dealt with.

a) What facts in the text suggest that the security precautions at Marignane airport were not strict enough? (Consider how the hi-jacker got aboard, and what he had with him.)

b) Why did the hi-jacker allow the plane to land again?

c) How did the security forces manage to gain access to the plane without the knowledge of the hi-jacker?

▲ *Fig. 9 LEAG*

GENERAL LEVEL

FRENCH LISTENING COMPREHENSION

Question 1 - You are at a railway station and hear the following loudspeaker announcement.

1. From which platform does the train leave? *(1 mark)*

....

Question 2 - You hear the following announcement at the railway station.

2. At what time is the train due to leave? *(1 mark)*

....

Question 3 - You are in an airport lounge and hear the following announcement.

3. Where are the passengers on flight 130 going to? *(1 mark)*

....

Question 4 - You want to catch a bus to the swimming pool. A passer-by gives you the following information.

4. When do the buses go? *(1 mark)*

....

Questions 5 and 6 - You have asked your way to the post office and are given the following directions.

5. Which direction should you take first? *(1 mark)*

....

6. Which direction should you take after the traffic lights? *(1 mark)*

....

▲ *Fig. 10 SEG*

Question one

You are at a railway station and hear the following loudspeaker announcement.

[Pause 5 seconds]

[M] Le train pour Rouen partira à 14.30, quai numéro 3.

[Pause 5 seconds]

[Repeat]

[Pause 10 seconds]

Question two

You hear the following announcement at the railway station.

[Pause 5 seconds]

[M] Attention! Attention! Le train express de 18h 15 en direction de Lyon va partir dans deux minutes, quai numéro six.

[Pause 5 seconds]

[Repeat]

[Pause 10 seconds]

Question three

You are in an airport lounge and hear the following announcement.

[Pause 5 seconds]

[F] Attention, les passagers du vol numéro 130, destination Nice. L'avion va décoller dans trente minutes à 16.45.

[Pause 5 seconds]

[Repeat]

[Pause 10 seconds]

Question four

You want to catch a bus to the swimming pool. A passer-by gives you the following information.

[Pause 5 seconds]

[F] Il vous faut - euh - le numéro 35. Il y a un car toutes les 10 minutes.

[Pause 5 seconds]

[Repeat]

[Pause 10 seconds]

Questions five and six

You have asked your way to the post office and are given the following directions.

[Pause 10 seconds]

[M] Eh bien, prenez la première rue à droite, continuez tout droit jusqu'aux feux puis tournez à gauche; la poste se trouve sur votre droite.

[Pause 15 seconds]

[Repeat]

[Pause 30 seconds]

▲ *Fig. 10 continued SEG Listening Comprehension Tapescript*

Fig. 11(a) NEA ►

Listen to these short conversations and, for each one, select, from List 1 below, the word that best describes the speaker's attitude and write it in the space provided (e.g. "He sounds furious.").

Find out as well what the conversation is about. Choose from List 2 below and write in the space provided (e.g. "The conversation is about missing the bus.")

LIST 1: ATTITUDES	
	furious
	sorry
	helpful
	worried
	disapproving
	grateful
	disappointed

LIST 2: TOPICS	
	missing the bus
	going out for the evening
	receiving a present
	broken crockery
	arriving late
	husband not being home yet
	doing the washing up
	repairing a puncture

(a) A woman is talking to her son's penfriend.

She sounds ______________________________

The conversation is about ______________________________

(b) A young woman is talking to her boyfriend.

She sounds ______________________________

The conversation is about ______________________________

(c) A mother is talking with her teenage daughter.

She sounds ______________________________

The conversation is about ______________________________

(d) A woman is talking with a friend at whose house she has just had a meal.

She sounds ______________________________

The conversation is about ______________________________

(e) A woman is talking to her neighbour.

She sounds ______________________________

The conversation is about ______________________________

(a) F: Oh, c'est pour moi? Oh, merci, que c'est gentil. Oh, vous n'auriez pas dû, monsieur. C'est de la part de vos parents? C'est vraiment aimable de leur part. Oh, que c'est gentil. C'est très, très joli. Il faudra que vous écris, que vous leur écriviez pour les remercier.

(b) F: Oh, je suis désolée. Ça fait longtemps que tu attends. Oh ...... vraiment, je sais pas, je, j'ai été prise dans un embouteillage, je suis vraiment désolée, j'espère que ...... le temps ne t'a pas paru trop long en attendant.

(c) F: Ah non, tu sais, sortir le soir, je crois que vraiment tu es un peu jeune. Et puis surtout au milieu de la semaine ...... demain matin, il faut que tu te lèves pour aller à l'école ...... et puis, vraiment, non. A ton âge, euh, moi, je sortais pas. Euh, non, je crois que vraiment tu attends encore un peu.

(d) F: Vous allez faire la vaisselle? Oh attendez un instant, je voudrais beaucoup vous aider.

(e) F: Je ne comprends pas ce qui se passe, il est, il est tard maintenant, euh, mon mari est, est vraiment en retard. Ça fait vingt minutes qu'il devrait être à la maison, je comprends vraiment pas. J'ai peur qu'il soit arrivé un accident, je ne sais pas ce que je pourrais faire. Je pourrais peut-être téléphoner ...... à la police, pour savoir s'il y a eu des accidents. Euh ...... oh, je sais pas vraiment.

1. A young French woman is coming to stay at your house. She rings to describe her appearance so that you can recognise her more easily.

   (a) Which train will she be arriving on?

   Answer: The train from ______________________ arriving in Charing Cross Station at ______________________ (TIME)

   (b) When the train arrives, you see these people waiting to be met. Which one fits her description?

   ____

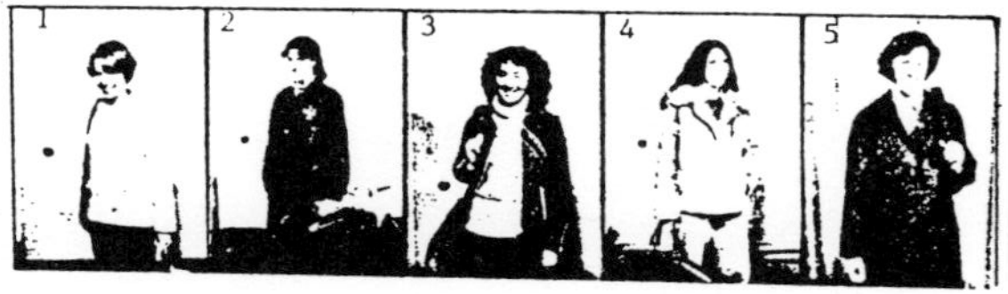

2. Things are not always straight-forward! You do not always receive the reply you expect, when you ask a question. In these short conversations, listen to the questions and spot what is UNEXPECTED in the replies. Write in the space provided.

   (a) In a shop, a woman asks for some slices of ham.

   ____

   (b) A woman arrives at an hotel.

   ____

   (c) A man asks the way in Paris.

   ____

   (d) One Friday evening, a man enquires about the time of the next plane to Lyon.

   ____

   (e) A man asks a woman for her 'phone number.

   ____

   (f) A young man checks on arrangements for going to the cinema tonight, with his girlfriend.

   ____

   (g) A woman asks a young man about his school subjects.

   ____

1. F: Allô? Euh, je suis la, la jeune femme qui va venir passer quelques jours chez vous. Je vous appelle pour, euh, pour, euh, nous mettre d'accord sur, euh, sur notre rendez-vous à la gare, hein? Je dois, je dois arriver par, euh, le train en provenance de Douvres, à sept heures et demie, à Charing Cross ...... et ...... mm, enfin, je pensais que peut-être il faudrait que je me décrive pour que ...... vous me reconnaissiez. Alors, sans doute, euh, je porterai une, euh, une valise, une petite valise rouge en cuir et je porterai sûrement, euh, je ne sais pas, un imperméable sans doute, un imperméable vert, vert foncé ...... et puis sûrement un parapluie aussi. Je suis de taille moyenne avec des cheveux bruns. Euh, je pense que vous me reconnaîtrez.

2.

(a) F: Bonjour, monsieur.

M: Bonjour, mademoiselle.

F: Je voudrais 4 tranches de jambon, s'il vous plaît.

M: 4 tranches de jambon ...... Euh, j'ai seulement de jambon en boîte, mademoiselle.

(b) F: Je voudrais une chambre avec salle de bains, s'il vous plaît.

M: Je suis désolé, nous sommes complets. Essayez à l'hôtel d'en face.

(c) M: Pardon, madame. Pour aller à la Tour Eiffel en métro, s'il vous plaît?

F: Je ne sais pas du tout, je ne suis pas d'ici.

(d) M: Mademoiselle, s'il vous plaît, le prochain avion pour Lyon?

F: Ah, je regrette, monsieur. Il n'y a pas d'avion avant lundi.

(e) M: Quel est votre numéro de téléphone, madame?

F: Ah, je regrette, je n'ai pas le téléphone.

(f) M: C'est toujours d'accord pour aller au cinéma ce soir?

F: Ah non, je peux vraiment pas, j'ai mal à la tête.

(g) F: Tu fais quelle matière à l'école?

M: Mais je ne vais plus à l'école depuis deux ans. Je travaille dans un supermarché.

▲ *Fig. 11(b) NEA – Questions and transcript*

(a) Rôle-Play One

You are in a post office in France. Your examiner will play the part of the counter-clerk.

Your tasks are:

to greet the clerk,
to post a parcel,
to buy stamps,
to enquire where the letter-box is,
to say thank you and goodbye.

(b) Rôle-Play Two

This is your first day in a French family. Ask your host or hostess:

the time of breakfast,
where to put your money and passport,
if you can phone your parents,
what the plans are for tomorrow,
to speak more slowly please.

(c) Guided Conversation

Personal information. To include topics: personal identity/age/family/home/school/interests.

Sample questions, e.g.:

Vous avez des frères ou des soeurs?

Où est-ce que vous habitez?

(Est-ce) c'est près de l'école?

Parlez-moi de votre école .....

Qu'est-ce que vous avez fait hier soir?

Qu'est-ce que vous aimez faire au week-end?

Avez-vous visité la France? (quel pays, quelle région de l'Angleterre avez-vous visité?)

Racontez-moi votre visite .....

▲ *Fig. 12(a) SEG Specimen Questions General Level*

The plan printed below gives an outline of a trip to France last summer.

Tell the Examiner about the journey and what happened on it. You need not mention every detail of the outline on the page and you can, for example, decide whether it was you who made the trip or someone you know.

Be prepared to respond to any questions or observations the Examiner might make.

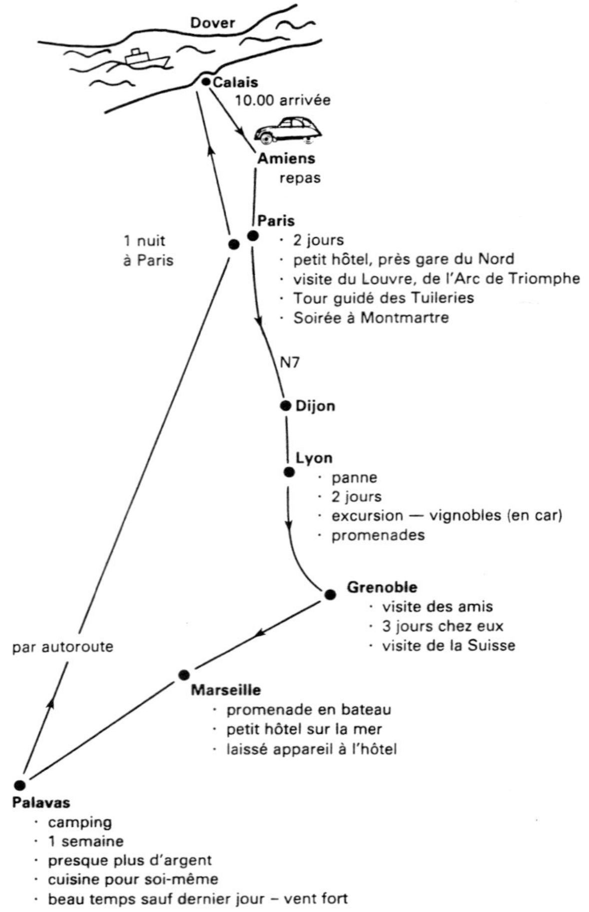

Fig. 12(b) MEG ▶

GRUGA PARK

Gruga · Vogelpark
Botanischer Garten

Kulshammerweg 32 · 4300 Essen 1 · Telefon (02 01) 88 · 78 07

EINTRITTSPREISE

Tageskarten:	**März – Oktober**	**November – Februar**
● Erwachsene	DM 3.00	DM 1.00
● Erwachsene ab 19.00 Uhr (April – September)	DM 1.50	
● Kinder/Jugendliche (6 - 17 Jahre)	DM 1.00	DM 0.50
● Kinder unter 6 Jahren in Begleitung eines Erwachsenen	frei	frei

ÖFFNUNGSZEITEN

Sommersaison

April bis Sept. 8.00 bis 24.00 Uhr – Kassenschluß 20.30 Uhr

Wintersaison:

Oktober bis März 9.00 Uhr bis zum Eintritt der Dunkelheit
Kassenschluß 16.30 Uhr

Gaststätten im Grugapark

Grugabad	Tel. 79 39 31	Cafeteria	Tel. 77 84 36
Landhaus	Tel. 77 96 12	Schänke am Tierhof	Tel. 78 84 04

Diverse Verkaufsstände im Park

Rollstuhl-Ausleihe an den Erste-Hilfe-Stationen:
Haupteingang Telefon 88-78 88 · Rollschuhbahn Telefon 88-78 89.

JULI

SA. 5. 7. 15–18 Uhr Musikpavillon	**Mit Pauken und Trompeten** Es spielt das Bundesbahn-Orchester und die Blizza-Harmonica-Gang
SO. 6. 7. 15–18 Uhr Musikpavillon	**Tanznachmittag** mit der Fred Sellman Big Band
FR. 11. 7. 9–18 Uhr Tummelwiese	**Frisbee-Golf** Europameisterschaft Veranstalter: Deutscher Frisbee Sport-Flugscheiben Verband
SA. 12. 7. 15–18 Uhr Musikpavillon	**Ein guter Sound** gespielt von der Gruppe Musik-Transfer
18.30 Uhr Musikpavillon	**Abendgottesdienst** Weigle-Haus · Essen
9–18 Uhr Tummelwiese	**Frisbee-Golf** Europameisterschaft
SO. 13. 7. 15–18 Uhr Musikpavillon	**Melodien aus Oper und Operette** Aufführung mit dem Theater und dem Philharmonischen Orchester Essen
9–18 Uhr Tummelwiese	**Frisbee-Golf** Europameisterschaft
SA. 19. 7. 15–18 Uhr Musikpavillon	**Zigeunerklänge** mit dem „Trio Farfarello" und den „Les Gitanes Swing"
SO. 20. 7. 15–18 Uhr Musikpavillon	**Musizierende Jugend** Bunter Nachmittag mit dem Schönebecker Jugendblas-Orchester und dem 1. Essener Akkordeon-Orchester
Sa. 26. 7. 15–18 Uhr Musikpavillon	**... noch einmal** mit der Peter Weisheit Band
SO. 27. 7. 15–18 Uhr Musikpavillon	**Mit Musik geht's besser** Unterhaltung mit den Siegtaler Musikanten

VERANSTALTUNGS PROGRAMM 86

Park und Verwaltung sind mit Straßenbahn, Bus und U-Bahn zu erreichen.
Straßenbahnlinie: 111
Haltestelle: Gruga
Von Mai bis Oktober, täglich im 10-Minuten-Takt.
Buslinien: 142 und 152 aus Richtung Kettwig
149 aus Richtung Wuppertal
Haltestelle: Alfred-Brücke
Diese Busse fahren ebenfalls im 10-Minuten-Takt.

Grugabad
Räumlich in den Park einbezogen, aber für Besucher abgetrennt, liegt das Grugabad. Es ist eines der größten und schönsten Freibäder Deutschlands.

Questions 1-5, which are set for General Level candidates, *must* be asked. The remainder are given as a guide to the type of question to be put to Extended Level candidates. If these actual questions are not used the examiner will substitute questions of a similar standard and type. Questions should require some manipulation of the text by the candidate, not merely the answers 'yes' or 'no'. Not all the questions will necessarily be used for each candidate.

1. Was kostet der Eintritt im Winter?
2. Ist der Park am Abend offen? (Bis wann?)
3. Ab wieviel Uhr (ab wann) ist der Eintritt billiger?
4. Wo kann man ein Glas Bier (oder eine Tasse Kaffee) trinken?
5. Wann (in welchem Monat) beginnt der Wintersaison?
6. Warum ist im Winter der Eintritt nach 16.30 Uhr nicht möglich?
7. Wo kann man Vögel sehen?
8. Wann ist der Eintritt im Sommer billiger?
9. Was kann man am 6. Juli machen?
10. Wohin würdest du gehen, wenn du Frisbee-Golf sehen möchtest?
11. Für wen kostet es nichts, in den Park zu kommen?
12. Können Kinder den Park immer besuchen?
13. Was für andere Möglichkeiten gibt es im Grugapark?
14. Was verstehst du unter 'Grugabahn'?
15. Kannst du mir etwas Information über das Grugabad geben?
16. Wie fährst du am besten zum Grugapark (, wenn du kein Auto hast)?
17. Wo und wann kann man die Peter Weisheit Band hören?
18. Was kostet der Eintritt für einen Vierzehnjährigen?
19. Im Grugapark gibt es eine Gaststätte, die Grugabad heißt. Warum, meinst du, heißt ein Gasthaus eigentlich Gruga*bad*?

▲ *Fig. 12(c) MEG*

▼ *Fig. 13 GCSE Orals*

	LEAG	MEG	NEA	SEG	WJEC
BASIC	2 role plays (3 + 5 utterances) Guided conversation (1 of 3 themes chosen 1 month earlier)	2 role plays Conversation (16 questions on at least 5 topic areas)	3 role plays (3 utterances each) General conversation	2 role plays (3 + 5 utterances) Guided conversation Questions on written/ visual stimulus	2 role plays Unprepared questions on 5 topic areas
HIGHER	2 role plays (basic 1 higher-level role play Guided conversation General conversation	*Part 1* 2 role plays (basic) 1 higher-level role play General conversation (basic or higher) *Part 2* As Part 1, plus narration of incident	3 role plays (basic) 2 higher-level role plays General conversation	2 role plays (basic) 1 higher-level role play (visual stimulus) Conversation (basic and higher) Questions on written/ visual stimulus Basic-level questions and higher-level too.	Basic oral plus 2 further role plays General conversation
CONDUCT AND ASSESSMENT	Conducted, recorded and assessed by the teacher. Tapes to be made available to the board's assessors, with moderation as necessary in the interests of standardisation. Oral tests to be taken in the summer term *within the exam period.*	Conducted by the teacher and *either* assessed at the time (with recording of candidates selected by the board *or* recordings of all candidates sent off for assessment. Tests to take place in *2–3 month period before* main exam period.	Conducted and recorded by the teacher and *assessed by the board's examiners.* No indication of examining period.	Conducted, assessed and recorded by the teacher; tapes sent off for moderation. No indication of examining period.	Conducted, assessed and recorded by the teacher; tapes sent off for moderation. No indication of examining period.

GENERAL LEVEL

FRENCH WRITING TEST

Answer BOTH questions.

1. Imagine that you are staying with a French penfriend. You have just answered the phone and promised to give a message to your friend, who is out at present. You want to go out too, so you leave a message on the message pad.

   Write a note in French saying:

   Who telephoned.

   Where he/she would like to go this evening.

   When he/she will phone again. *(6 marks)*

2. Write a letter in French, of 70/80 words, to the hotel in this advertisement, including the points below:

BAR RESTAURANT 29110 CONCARNEAU

HOTEL DE LA PLAGE

☆☆☆

CHAMBRES TOUT CONFORT OUVERT TOUTE L'ANNEE

(a) Give the dates when you want to stay at the hotel.

(b) Say you want one double and one single room.

(c) Say whether you want a bathroom or a shower.

(d) Ask if the hotel is near the beach.

(e) Ask if there is a disco at the hotel.

(f) Ask if there is a car park.

Remember to start, date and end the letter correctly. *(20 marks)*

▲ *Fig. 14(a) SEG Specimen Questions General Level*

Question 1

You have sent your name and address to an agency in France which was advertising for English teenagers to write to French children of the same age, and they have sent you the following form to fill in. Answer each point IN FRENCH giving details of your family, school subjects and interests as requested.

Nom .... Prénom ....

Age .... ans .... mois

Famille...

....

....

Etudes

Matières étudiées à l'école ....

....

Langues parlées ....

Intérêts

Sports préférés ....

Autres intérêts ....

....

Date ....

▲ *Fig. 14(b) LEAG*

Your French friend is on holiday and has sent you this postcard:

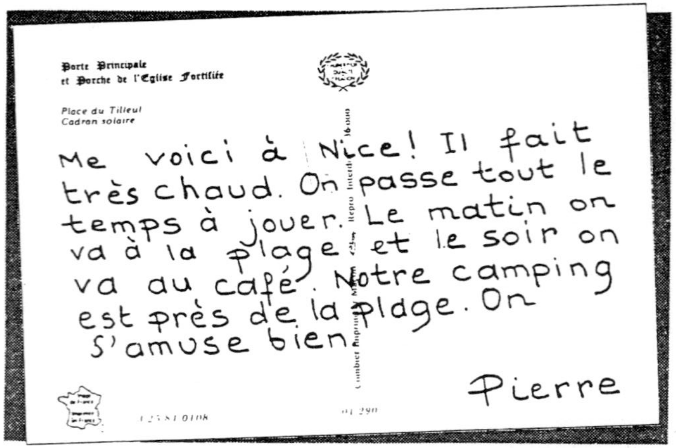
Porte Principale
et Porche de l'Eglise Fortifiée
Place du Tilleul
Cadran solaire
Me voici à Nice! Il fait très chaud. On passe tout le temps à jouer. Le matin on va à la plage et le soir on va au café. Notre camping est près de la plage. On s'amuse bien.
Pierre

When you go on holiday to Scarborough you write a similar postcard in French back to your friend. But in Scarborough the weather is cold, you go to a disco in the evenings and you are staying in a hotel near the beach.

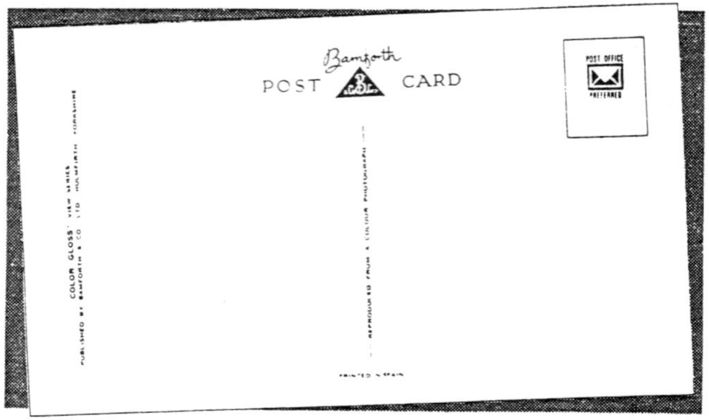
Bamforth
POST CARD
POST OFFICE
PREFERRED

▲ *Fig. 14(c) NEA*

1. A youth orchestra from Caen is planning to visit your district and give some performances. You have been asked by the organisers to help by writing (in French) to confirm arrangements.

Using the 3 documents below as a starting point, write a letter of about 100 words:

(a) Acknowledging Mme. Hervé's letter and telegram,

(b) Confirming that the group is now expected on Thursday 16th July at 7.00 p.m.,

(c) Saying you are enclosing a programme,

(d) Giving more details of the 3 activities underlined in document 3,

(e) Wishing them a pleasant journey.

DOCUMENT 1 — Caen, le 30 juin 1985

Chers amis,

Je suis heureuse de vous annoncer que les préparatifs pour la visite de nos jeunes musiciens sont maintenant complets.

Nous espérons arriver (en car) le mercredi, quinze juillet, au début de la soirée. Je vous communiquerai l'heure précise de notre arrivée dans quelques jours.

Nous attendons avec impatience d'être parmi vous, et de faire la connaissance des familles qui ont gentiment proposé de nous loger.

En attendant le quinze, je vous remercie vivement de tous les soins que vous avez pris pour assurer le succès de cette visite.

Avec mes plus sincères amitiés.

Madeleine Hervé (Mme)

DOCUMENT 2 - Text of message received by telegram on 8th July

REGRETTONS CHANGEMENT DE PLAN INEVITABLE. ORCHESTRE ARRIVE JEUDI 16 JUILLET 19.00 HRS. M. HERVE

DOCUMENT 3 - Visit of Youth Orchestra from Caen: Outline Programme

Thursday	16/7	Evening	Arrival at Bus Station. Evening with families.
Friday	17/7	Morning	Reception at Town Hall (11.30 - 12.15).
"		Afternoon	Rehearsal (2.00 p.m.)
"		Evening	First concert - Church Hall (7.30 p.m.)
Saturday	18/7	Afternoon	Coach tour and Picnic Lunch (12.00 noon - 5.00 p.m.)
"		Evening	Youth Club Disco (8.30 - 11.45 p.m.)
Sunday	19/7	Morning	Rehearsal (10.30 a.m.)
"		Afternoon	Second concert - Arts Centre (3.00 p.m.)
Monday	20/7		Free for shopping, sight-seeing, etc.
"		Evening	Farewell party for visitors and families (8.00 p.m.)
Tuesday	21/7	Morning	Departure from Bus Station (10.15 a.m. prompt)

▲ *Fig. 15(a) SEG Specimen Question Extended Level*

Salut

Je te remercie beaucoup de la lettre qui m'a fait grand plaisir.

Ouf! c'est bientôt la fin de l'année, je suis en vacances le 9 juin car mon Lycée est un centre d'examens.

L'année a été dure, je dois me lever tous les matins à 7h. moins le quart pour prendre l'autobus de 8h. moins 20. A huit heures et quart, la classe commence. Chaque cours dure 55 minutes. J'ai cours de 8h. et quart à 12h10. Le matin, j'ai des cours comme les maths, le français, la physique, puis l'après-midi, de 2h. à 4 ou 5h. cela dépend des jours, j'ai l'anglais, l'espagnol le latin ou encore l'histoire ou la géographie. La journée est finie. Je rentre chez moi et travaille de 5h. et demie à 8h, et je travaille beaucoup le week-end. Au Lycée, les élèves sont libres. Nous pouvons nous habiller comme nous voulons, fumer et sortir du Lycée. L'important c'est d'être au cours, le reste n'a pas d'importance. Je ne fais presque pas de sport: 2h. par semaine avec l'école. Je faisais aussi du tennis, mais cette année je n'ai plus le temps.

Ne voyant plus grand-chose à te dire, je te quitte du stylo mais pas du coeur!

Véronique Molle

P.S Comment se passe une journée de classe en Angleterre?

Question 1 Write below a reply to the letter on the page opposite which you have received from your French penfriend. Describe your normal school day so that your penfriend can compare herself with you. Mention also something of interest you have done recently or are planning to do. Write approximately 100 words in French, excluding your address and the date.

▲ *Fig. 15(b) NEA*

Bild C

(g) Wo ist dieser Herr? (*½ mark*)

(h) Warum sieht er sich den Fahrplan an? (*2½ marks*)

Bild D

(i) Was macht der Polizist? (*1½ marks*)

(j) Warum tut er das? (*2½ marks*)

Bild E

(k) Was will die alte Dame tun? (*1½ marks*)

(l) Was tut der höfliche junge Mann? (*1½ marks*)

(m) Warum braucht die alte Dame seine Hilfe? (*1 mark*)

▲ *Fig. 15(c) NEA*

3 Differentiation and assessment

BENEFITS OF DIFFERENTIATION

Someone once said, cynically, that for modern languages the O level was a certificate of near incompetence, while the CSE was one of complete incompetence! Although this is clearly not the case, there are, nevertheless, a few grains of truth in the statement. This being so, the implications are interesting. If a candidate obtains a certificate but cannot show practical application of the knowledge gained, then the examination must be testing the wrong things. Similarly, if an examination shows incompetence – what the candidate cannot do – the candidates are judged by failure rather than by positive achievement.

The O level was intended only for the top 20–25 per cent of the ability range, and it was required that approximately 30 per cent of these should be awarded less than a Grade C, no matter how good pupils may have been. In a good year, with all candidates obtaining high marks, the grade thresholds would simply have been raised, ensuring that the percentage of grades awarded would remain constant. This was also the case with the CSE, and so differentiation between candidates was by degrees of failure rather than by attainment. In addition, the CSE was always regarded as second-best to O level, and indeed was taken by those pupils not in the top 20 per cent for the ability range. Grade 1 was never really regarded as a true equivalent to GCE grade C.

The GCSE will remove the O level/CSE divide, but the problem of designing an examination for a wide ability range still exists. The *General Criteria* (Section 9) state that the examination 'will be designed, not for any particular proportion of the ability range, but for all candidates, whatever their ability relative to other candidates, who are able to reach the standards required for the award of particular grades'. Therefore, with candidates of widely varying abilities, it is essential to devise schemes of differentiated assessment so that the examinations can 'demand more of able than less able candidates and to award grades accordingly' (General Introduction, paragraph 33).

Whereas the previous system often set tasks which were too difficult for most pupils and then measured the degree of failure, differentiation allows a range of tasks to be set at differing levels of achievement. This principle is set out in the General Introduction to GCSE (para. 33):

> Grades will be awarded as far as practicable on the basis of good performances, earning good marks, in tasks which stretch

> candidates at varying levels of ability while being within their reach, rather than on the basis of poor performance, earning low marks, in tasks which are unsuitable for them.

These tasks, then, should be set appropriately for different students' levels of attainment, so that success rather than failure is measured. This insistence on the positive aspect of assessment and on the idea of a common core onto which other elements can be added according to attainment and ability is a major step forward in examining at 16+.

Differentiation, therefore, helps to guard against two potential dangers: assessment tasks which are too difficult and therefore disheartening, with any marks being gained in random fashion; secondly, assessment tasks which are too easy, do not stretch the candidate and present no challenge. Both of these situations are demotivating. Furthermore the positive side of assessment comes to the fore in a 'bottom-up' approach which gives candidates due credit for attainment at basic level first, before testing the higher-level skills.

CATEGORIES OF DIFFERENTIATION

Differentiation by outcome

Within the context of the GCSE examination, there are five main categories to be considered. Firstly, there is differentiation by outcome, which is the technique of providing a 'neutral stimulus', i.e. one that is neutral with respect to difficulty. A picture, for example, can provide a stimulus which could lead to appropriate writing at all levels of ability. It is the manner in which the task is completed that creates the differentiation; thus there can be an assessment of process as well as product, which makes this particularly suitable for assessing coursework. It is important that clear guidelines are devised to enable worthwhile work at all levels to be credited.

Stepped questions

Although, in some subjects, all candidates may have covered the same ground, it is unreasonable to expect them all to reach the same level. In these cases, stepped questions offer a format for assessing separate abilities within a single context and they can also guide a candidate through a complex topic. The question is formulated in several parts, with each part in ascending order of difficulty and each carrying a separate mark (Fig. 1).

▼ *Fig. 1*

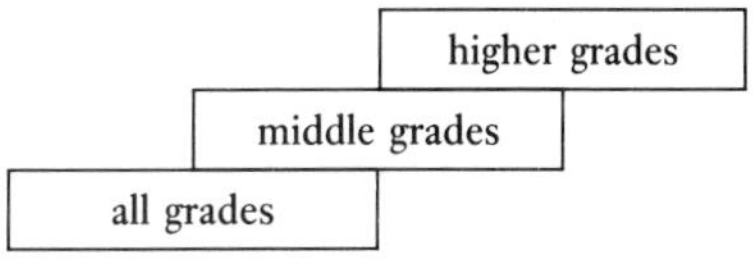

All candidates would attempt the early part of each question, with the more able showing what they can do by tackling the later parts. It is important to make sure that the earlier parts of each question provide a worthwhile task and that the less able candidates are purposefully engaged throughout the examination. A drawback here is that some candidates may feel that they have never satisfactorily completed a question, while the more able may feel that time is being wasted on the earlier parts.

Stepped papers

Stepped papers follow the same principle as above, except that here it is the paper itself which is graded, with questions arranged in ascending order of difficulty. Candidates attempt as many questions as they wish. A problem with this type of paper is whether, within the examination time-limits, enough assessment material for abler candidates can be included to give effective discrimination while still adequately testing the others, who are having to make important decisions about which question to answer under examination stress. There could also be the feeling of dissatisfaction for some at not finishing a paper, so that the experience would not necessarily be a positive one.

Differentiated sections

One way of avoiding this problem is to have papers with differentiated sections. The more difficult sections are attempted only by the more-able candidates. However, if such papers are used, then clear guidance must be given to pupils before the examination on which section to attempt. With both this and the previous category there is the danger of half the candidates sitting, twiddling their thumbs, waiting for the other half to finish.

Differentiated papers

In many subjects, particularly those which are 'sequential' in nature and where there are wide differences in the level pupils can cope with, differentiated papers have been recommended by subject-specific criteria. These are in mathematics, physics, chemistry, biology, science and languages. Here there are two or more levels of paper which correlate with particular grades as the following example (from mathematics) shows:

Level 1:	Papers 1–2 give access to grades	G	F	E				
Level 2:	Papers 2–3 give access to grades		F	E	D	C		
Level 3:	Papers 3–4 give access to grades				D	C	B	A

Thus, there are three levels of entry, and teachers will have to give careful thought to and advise on the level each candidate should attempt. Were a candidate to enter level 3, but gain insufficient marks to qualify for a grade D, then he or she would be awarded an ungraded certification. This puts great responsibility on the teacher for choosing the correct entry level, while being a useful weapon for resisting pressure to enter pupils at a level inappropriate to their attainment. This ensures that the examination tests attainment, i.e. what the pupil can do.

DIFFERENTIATION AND MODERN LANGUAGES

Differentiation in modern languages is achieved by a combination of various strategies, but mainly by differentiated papers. There are two levels of paper in each of the four separate skills of listening, reading, speaking and writing – basic and higher level. This holds true for all the examining groups, although MEG has sub-divided its higher-level into Parts 1 and 2, giving effectively three levels, while SEG has decided that the nomenclature of 'general' and 'extended' for the two levels is psychologically better for the candidates.

This division into two levels is clearly mirrored in the syllabuses, where the topics, structures and vocabularly lists are defined in terms of what is required at basic and higher level. Therefore at higher level a candidate would be expected to demonstrate knowledge of all items listed under basic, plus the additional items listed for the more advanced level, thus permitting for effective discrimination between the more and less able candidates.

As well as the higher level being more demanding than basic, there is also, within the levels, an element of stepped papers, showing an incline of difficulty from the first, easier questions to the harder, later ones. This is shown in Figures 2–5: Figures 2–4 are from the SEG's general-level reading paper (Questions 3, 7 and 13), and the incline of difficulty is clear. The fourth example (Figure 5, page 59) is from the NEA's higher-level reading paper which well illustrates the jump in difficulty between the two levels.

Finally, and most importantly, by using a building-block

3. This is an advert for a Walking Race.

(a) At what time does it start?

(b) Where does it finish?

(1 mark)

(1 mark)

DIMANCHE 5 SEPTEMBRE

16ème Grand prix international
de St-Nazaire (sur 6 heures)

A LA MARCHE

Départ 5 H. devant l'HOTEL DES POSTES
Arrivée 11 H. même endroit
- avec: L'Italie
Le Luxembourg
La Belgique
L'Angleterre
L'Espagne
L'Allemagne
et : 25 Clubs Français

▲ *Fig. 2 SEG Specimen Question General Level*

7. Here is a notice at the sea-side:

ATTENTION A LA MAREE MONTANTE

Il est dangereux de se baigner dans la mer aux heures de la marée montante qui peut vous surprendre à tout instant.

Renseignez-vous sur l'heure des marées en téléphonant au 98.52.03.68.

What is it dangerous to do when the tide is coming in? *(2 marks)*

▲ *Fig. 3 SEG Specimen Question General Level*

13. This is a cutting from a newspaper:

Quatre-vingt-cinq pour cent des Français restent en France pour leurs vacances. La plupart vont sur la côte, les autres vont ou à la montagne ou à la campagne. Pour les quinze pour cent qui vont à l'étranger, l'Espagne et le Portugal semblent être les pays les plus visités. Cependant, les pays d'Afrique du Nord, surtout le Maroc et la Tunisie deviennent de plus en plus populaires.

(a) Of the French people who stay in France for their holidays, **where** do most prefer to go? *(1 mark)*

(b) Which are the **two** most popular countries visited? *(1 mark)*

▲ *Fig. 4 SEG Specimen Question General Level*

system, the national criteria for French have created a form of differentiation in the entry pattern of the examination for all languages (Figure 6).

There is an obligatory common core of basic reading, listening and speaking, following which candidates may enter for any, or all, of the other elements of the examination as appropriate to their level of attainment. However, in the entry pattern, these higher elements of the examination are linked in specific ways to the higher grades and, therefore, candidates not offering certain combinations of elements may not have access to the highest grades. The requirements for the different grades are summarised in the *National Criteria* (3.3.3) as follows:

Grades G, F and E	:	three common-core elements
Grade D	:	three common-core elements + any one additional element
Grade C	:	three common-core elements + basic writing + any one higher-level additional element
Grade B	:	three common-core elements + basic writing + higher-level writing + any one additional higher-level element
Grade A	:	three common-core + basic writing + higher level writing + any two additional higher-level elements.

4. Un Soldat du Contingent: Robert

Read this article from a young people's magazine about the after effects on a soldier who went to fight in the Algerian war of independence with France. Then answer the questions below, in English, basing your answers on the article.

UN SOLDAT DU CONTINGENT: ROBERT

Deux millions de soldats français ont participé à la guerre d'Algérie entre 1954 et 1962. Robert a passé vingt-sept mois là-bas, dans la ville qu'habitait Josette.

Mais il n'a jamais tiré un coup de feu. Pendant plus de deux ans, il est resté dans la même caserne. Il faisait un travail spécial, secret, ennuyeux. Il s'occupait des renseignements. Ce service s'occupait de savoir où se cachaient les Arabes armés. Lui, Robert, recevait des renseignements, téléphonait, transmettait des ordres. Il ne parlait pas aux Arabes, il ne comprenait pas ce qu'il venait faire dans ce pays chaud.

Ses chefs lui donnaient du vin gratuitement. Du vin pour vaincre la soif, l'ennui. Robert ne sortait jamais de la caserne. Une fois revenu en France, Robert a continué à boire. Il a perdu son travail, n'en a pas retrouvé.

Robert pense que la vie est une vraie cochonnerie. Il est malade, désabusé. Il vit seul. Depuis vingt ans qu'il est revenu d'Algérie, il n'a plus le goût de vivre. Il parle par petites phrases: 'Ah, les vaches, si tu savais, quelle connerie, tout ça!"

Que faudrait-il savoir? Qu'est-ce que Robert cache an fond de lui et qu'il n'arrive pas à oublier?

(a) How long was Robert in Algeria for?

____

(b) What sort of work was he involved in?

A. interesting work
B. distribution of weapons
C. locating Arab soldiers
D. translating Arabic

Answer (letter only): ☐

(c) What did he receive free of charge?

A. information
B. wine
C. phone calls home
D. a radio

Answer (letter only): ☐

(d) When he got back to France what was he unable to do?

A. drink wine
B. stop working
C. go out alone
D. keep a job

Answer (letter only): ☐

(e) When the article was written, how long had he been back in France?

____

(f) What effect did his Algerian experience have on his life as a whole?

A. He lost all interest in life.
B. He was a lot happier.
C. It made him sympathise with the Algerians.
D. It made him forgetful.

Answer (letter only): ☐

▲ *Fig. 5 NEA*

▼ *Fig. 6*

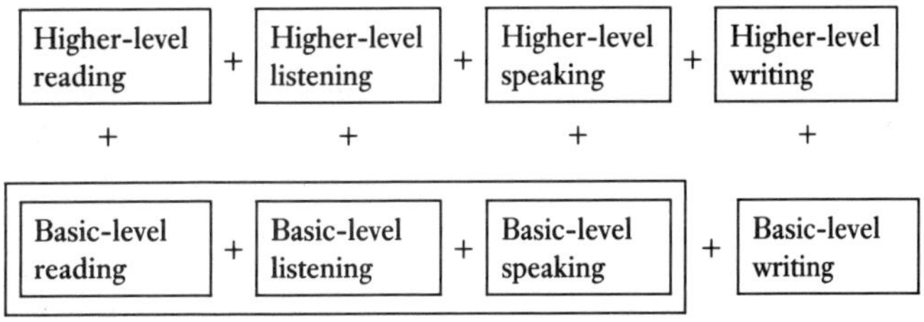

The positive aspect of these requirements is that they present teachers with the flexibility to tailor examination entry to the attainment level of each individual pupil. The examination then becomes a positive experience for the candidates, where they can successfully answer questions, instead of one where they are obliged to tackle tasks beyond their ability and thus experience failure. This is the spirit of the GCSE. However, teachers should note that, by choosing certain combinations, they are putting a definite ceiling on what grade a candidate can obtain. To enter a pupil for the three common-core elements means a ceiling of grade E, however well he or she may perform in these elements.

The role of writing

Writing acts as a hurdle for grades C and above. In order to obtain a grade C, basic writing must be attempted, so that a candidate who attempts basic- and higher-level reading, listening and speaking is limited to D, while one who attempts the four skills at basic level plus one additional element (say, reading) can be awarded a C. However, it is perhaps reasonable to expect a candidate who can successfully attempt the higher level in three skill areas to be able to cope with basic writing. It is less reasonable to insist on higher-level writing for grade B, since a pupil who performs well at the four basic skills plus three higher-level elements, excluding writing, is surely worth this grade. Not every grade A/B student will continue with languages at undergraduate level!

Entry combinations

The building-block system, although designed to give flexibility and a wide choice of entry, has nevertheless presented teachers with a complicated entry pattern and considerable implications for organisation. Modern languages have more possible entry combinations than any other subject. Whereas drama has sixteen, mathematics three and English two, modern languages have twenty-four possible entry combinations. Figure 7 demonstrates how these combinations can be formed.

The problem will be how to choose the correct entry point for each pupil. Will it mean that teachers will choose the point which demands least (in their opinion) for a particular grade – for example at No. 2 instead of 9? Or will it encourage schools to enter pupils for inappropriate elements as an 'insurance policy' and incline parents to put pressure on teachers to enter their offspring for everything on the grounds that 'you can't lose, can you?' None of this is in the spirit of an examination which requires candidates to earn their marks 'in tasks which stretch (them) ... while being within their reach, rather than on the

▼ *Fig. 7 Possible entry combinations for a modern language*

No. of Entry	Basic level					Higher level			Highest possible grade
	Read	Listen	Speak	Write	Read	Listen	Speak	Write	
1	×	×	×						E
2	×	×	×	×					
3	×	×	×		×				
4	×	×	×			×			
5	×	×	×				×		D
6	×	×	×		×	×			
7	×	×	×		×		×		
8	×	×	×			×	×		
9	×	×	×		×	×	×		
10	×	×	×	×	×				
11	×	×	×	×		×			
12	×	×	×	×			×		
13	×	×	×	×				×	C
14	×	×	×	×	×	×			
15	×	×	×	×	×		×		
16	×	×	×	×		×	×		
17	×	×	×	×	×	×	×		
18	×	×	×	×	×			×	
19	×	×	×	×		×		×	B
20	×	×	×	×			×	×	
21	×	×	×	×	×	×	×		
22	×	×	×	×	×		×	×	A
23	×	×	×	×		×	×	×	
24	×	×	×	×	×	×	×	×	

basis on poor performances, earning low marks, in tasks which are unsuitable to them' (op.cit.).

Yet it is clearly unreasonable to present teachers with such a range of entry points with the anomalies that they contain. How can it be argued that No. 10 is necessarily better than 9, or 18 than 17? This complexity is certainly due, in part, to the decision to test all four skills discretely at two levels, since, were there to be more integrated skills testing or a greater coursework element with mixed-skill tasks, then this situation could be changed.

However, the worry is that such a complicated system could be self-defeating. With so many possible entry patterns, it could mean that within one teaching group there is a wider range of examination requirements than hitherto experienced. This gives rise to problems of setting – whether in wider-ability groups than previously or in more homogeneous sets. Concomitant with this is the effect the ability range may have on teaching styles. Some schools may avoid the issue by simply entering candidates either for just the four basic elements or all basic and higher elements, thus reproducing, in a fashion, the old two-tier system.

It is obvious that the suggested range of entry points need to be rationalised so that schools will keep the flexibility to allow schools to enter pupils appropriately, but teachers will not be presented with an unmanageable system. Therefore, bearing in mind the statement in the *National Criteria – French* which point out that 'in every case the overall level of competence required over the elements listed would be very high and that candidates with realistic prospects of gaining the grade would normally offer a greater number of elements than the minimum requirement', the five-point scale of entry in Figure 8 is a suggested solution.

▼ *Fig. 8 Suggested five-point scale of entry*

No. of Entry	Basic level					Higher level			Highest possible grade
	Read	Listen	Speak	Write	Read	Listen	Speak	Write	
1	×	×	×						E
2	×	×	×	×					D
3	×	×	×		×	×			
4	×	×	×	×	×	×	(×)		C
5	×	×	×	×	×	×	×	×	A

The suggested scale would offer simplicity and also the flexibility to cover a wide range of ability without submitting pupils to inappropriate tasks. Entry points 2 and 3 give the opportunity of obtaining a grade D with or without writing. The assumption is that at entry point 3, where only one additional element is necessary, candidates can cope with both reading and listening at higher level. Entry points 3 and 4 would correlate well with the MEG higher-level Part 1.

In this scheme, there is a clear indication for ability grouping or setting at three levels within the languages department, since mixed-ability groups at fourth- and fifth-year level do not provide for the most efficient and successful teaching. Candidates entering at points 1 and 2 could reasonably be taught together, as could 3 and 4. This also has the advantage of giving the better ones in each grouping the possibility of moving up a grade.

There is also an argument for grouping together entry points 1 and 3 and 2 and 4. This would give access to higher grades by extension of the skills being practised at basic level insted of the additional skill of writing being added for some pupils within the same group, which could be seen as divisive, and which would make teaching easier. Candidates entering at point 5 would be the top set of able linguists – those who form the bulk of our present O level groups.

OVERALL GRADING

▼ *Fig. 9 The points-to-grade scale*

	Points	Grade	Points	
SEG NEA LEAG WJEC	24–28	A	27–32	MEG
	21–23	B	23–26	
	18–20	C	19–22	
	14–17	D	15–18	
	10–13	E	10–14	
	5–9	F	5–9	
	1–4	G	1–4	

The building-block system also presents a problem with the final overall grading, since achievement in eight possible papers at different levels in various combinations has to be unified into one overall grade. This is being achieved in various ways, all of which will be published separately by the different consortia, but basically each candidate will be awarded up to seven points in each individual skill attempted (except by the Midland Examining Group, where it will be eight). Thus, a candidate performing excellently in all four skills at basic and higher levels would score a total of $4 \times 7 = 28$ points. A candidate entering the three basic core elements, but doing well in them, might score $3 \times 4 = 12$ points. Another might score 5 for reading, 6 for listening, 4 for speaking and 3 for writing, giving a total of 18.

The MEG, because of its two-part higher-level Examination, awards 4 points for basic, 2 for higher level Part 1, and 2 for higher-level Part 2, thus giving a total of 8 possible points for each skill and a total possible global score of 32 points. These total scores are then referred to a points-to-grade scale recommended by the Secondary Examinations Council (Figure 9). Therefore our first candidate would be awarded an A, the second an E and the third a C. One criticism of these scales has been the unequal spread of points to grades in the 28-point scale, which many lead to bunching in the middle grades.

The way the consortia arrive at the points differs. As examples, we can look at both NEA and SEG. With NEA, each test or paper will be marked according to the detailed mark scheme, as published with the specimen papers. On the basis of the total marks scored, a candidate will be awarded points on a scale of 0–4 at basic and 0–3 at higher level as shown in Figure 10.

▼ *Fig. 10 NEA mark scheme*

Higher	Listening	Reading	Speaking	Writing
	3	3	3	3
	2	2	2	2
	1	1	1	1
	0	0	0	0
Basic	**Listening**	**Reading**	**Speaking**	**Writing**
	4	4	4	4
	3	3	3	3
	2	2	2	2
	1	1	1	1
	0	0	0	0

For candidates taking basic and higher levels in any skill area, the points scored at basic level are added to those scored at higher level. The criteria used to determine the award of points are described in detail in the syllabus. For example, in reading, the criteria are as shown in Figure 11. The points obtained for all four skills are then aggregated and the total is translated into a grade using the scale in Figure 9. This system of marking follows the spirit of the new examination, as it is positive and gives credit for what pupils can do.

▼ *Fig 11 Criteria for awarding points for reading*

Basic

0 Consistently fails to demonstrate understanding of relevant details in the material presented.
1 Able to demonstrate understanding of some common instructions, signs and notices on public display.
2 Able to demonstrate understanding of common instructions, signs and notices on public display, and to extract some relevant specific information from such texts as simple brochures, guides and letters.
3 Able to demonstrate understanding of instructions, signs and notices on public display, and to extract most of the relevant specific information from such texts as simple brochures, guides, letters and other forms of appropriate continuous writing, including imaginative writing.
4 Able to demonstrate understanding of instructions, signs and notices on public display, and to extract all or almost all relevant specific information from such texts as simple brochures, guides, letters and other form of appropriate writing, including imaginative writing.

Higher

0 Fails to demonstrate the qualities required for higher level.
1 Able to extract important information from short or extended texts.
2 Able to identify some of the important points or themes of short or extended texts and to draw some conclusions from such texts.
3 Able to identify most of the important points or themes in extended texts, to draw conclusions from and to identify relationships in such texts.

The SEG system

The SEG has a different and rather more complicated system, but nevertheless one which sets out to give credit for what a candidate can do. An important difference from other consortia is that, within the skills, there is an overlap between basic and higher level. Whereas in the NEA the proportion of points between the two levels is 4:3, in the SEG it is 5:4. The *National Criteria* (para. 5.2) suggest that basic level is directed at four grades, D–G, and higher level at three grades, A–C, but SEG felt that candidates performing well on basic-level papers could achieve C grades on components representing positive achievement, and that fewer higher-level papers would have to be taken, which could lead to negative experiences. This explains why an apparently slightly more difficult list of structures for active use appears in the SEG languages syllabuses. Within SEG, all subjects with differentiated papers have this overlap.

Adjusting the marks

When all marking according to the detailed schemes in the syllabus is complete, a grading panel will make qualitative judgements based on the work of the candidates to arrive at the mark boundaries for G/F, D/C and B/A in each skill. For basic level, the first two, G/F and D/C, have to be made and for higher level, the second two, D/C and B/A. Other grade boundaries will be calculated by a computer. Candidates entered for basic level only will then be awarded a grade, up to and including C, according to their marks. For candidates taking basic plus higher level in any skill, the performances will have to be combined by adjusting the marks so that the papers have equal weight and then adding together the two scores. For example, if reading is out of 50 at basic and 60 at higher level, then basic marks have to be multiplied by $^6/_5$ before being added to the higher marks. So if a candidate scores $^{40}/_{50}$ at basic, scaled up, that becomes $^{48}/_{60}$, which would be added to a higher-level mark of, say, $^{45}/_{60}$, giving a total of $^{93}/_{120}$. By combining the C/D grade boundaries at basic and higher levels in such a way as to give equal weighting and establishing the other grade boundaries, grades for each skill can now be awarded. This can be converted into points (7 for A, 6 for B etc.), aggregated, and a global, overall grade awarded according to the points-to-grade scale.

Although appearing complicated, it is a system which advantages the average candidate who has mastered the basic skills, since candidates who do not gain enough marks on the aggregate of their basic- and higher-level performance to gain at least grade D will be given the grade awarded on the basic paper only, which could well be a C. A candidate who obtains D on basic and higher, because of a poor higher-level performance, but a C on the basic paper, will be awarded C overall. There is one disadvantage in that overall grades arrived at in this way may have to be modified according to the requirements of the national criteria. This may cause problems for the SEG, but also indicates that the national criteria should also in future revise these grade requirements.

It is important that teachers acquaint themselves with the grading systems of the the consortia, since this may help in the decision on which consortium to choose, as the examinations themselves have a broad similarity in format and content. The way in which tests are marked has an effect on classroom practice.

IMPLICATIONS FOR TEACHERS

Pupil profiling

Firstly, the emphasis on differentiation and flexible entry pattern puts a far greater focus on the learner, and if candidates are to be entered correctly, then this calls for some system of profiling. Teachers must be able to make professional judgements on the level of attainment of their pupils and to be able to justify these judgements. There must be clear reasons why a pupil is entered for particular elements of the examinations and not others. A system of profiling is also a yardstick for progress and will give pupils valuable information about their own learning.

Schemes of work

Thought must be given to schemes of work, particularly, but not only, for years 4 and 5, to ensure that they fit into the demands and requirements of the new examination. It will be necessary, for example, to make certain that all four of the skill areas are adequately provided for and that the emphasis is not still on, say, written work. Reading is perhaps a neglected skill, but will need to be practised, as will the other skills, but in a balanced fashion. Similarly a scheme of work must make sure that all the topic areas are covered. However, since many of these, or many aspects of them, will have been taught during the first two or three years of learning the language, the problem has to be tackled of how to recycle these topics at different levels without provoking the rather too familiar cry of: 'We did this last year – and the year before ...'

Teacher time and resources

Another implication is in the use of teacher time. The emphasis on authentic materials linked to appropriate and relevant language tasks means that more time will be needed for preparation, and ways have to be explored in which teachers can be helped to produce new material when their time and money are inevitably limited. Obviously, a foreign-language assistant, if available, can from time to time be better used in preparing materials instead of taking small groups and, within LEAs, some sort of central resource bank could be set up to share work done in schools.

Most importantly, though, there has to be teamwork within departments so that teachers can work together, sharing ideas, materials and preparation of materials – for example, the exploitation of a text by a range of graded exercises (not necessarily written), varied worksheets and tasks. This leads inevitably to resources and to the consideration of a more eclectic approach rather than adhering to one particular textbook. There is a wide range of material available, from published books to television, radio, newspapers, magazines and photographs. How these resources are used is of paramount importance, and departments should be considering ideas for a communicative approach, particularly from the field of teaching English as a Foreign Language, where much interesting work has been done.

Schemes of work, resources and approaches in the classroom are all dealt with in greater detail in later chapters.

Teaching languages as a means of communication rather than just an exercise in linguistic manipulation should mean more time spent in the classroom on pair or group-work and in setting up situations with an information gap, thereby providing a genuine purpose for talking, reading, listening or writing. However, the important point must once again be made: language itself is not a discrete skill activity, and this should be mirrored in classroom practice. Within the classroom, the skills must be integrated with, for example, reading leading to talking leading to writing.

Assessing pupil performance: efficient and constructive marking

However, this brings us to a final, important implication for teachers: that of assessing pupil performance within the classroom, including, of course, tasks set for homework. It is perhaps correct to assume that most assessment of pupils' work is in the form of homework, and therefore written. It is also fair to assume that teachers spend a great deal of time after school on this task, underlining mistakes, writing in the correct version and transferring books from piles of uncorrected ones into piles of marked ones. After two or three hours' work they have the impression of having worked hard and productively. Hard certainly, but how productively is questionable.

A great deal of marking is dull, boring, often inconsequential and time-consuming! Too much effort is spent on marking written work, which has little effect on learning, and not enough on preparation which is essential for good classroom practice. This is not to say that written work should not be marked – indeed it should, although not necessarily every piece – but ways should be found to cut down on time spent. One method may be to use a system of symbols – S for spelling, T for tense, W for word-order etc. – so that mistakes in the written language are pointed out and a clue given about the type of error. This is certainly quicker than writing in corrections above mistakes.

There must be an insistence on pupils producing a corrected version, which makes them think about their mistakes, hence aiding the learning process. Otherwise, they are only interested in the mark at the bottom, which usually tells them little other than that they obtained a higher or lower mark than their neighbour, and they do not learn from the process, since the work, the correction of mistakes, has been done for them.

Bearing in mind this last point, we should consider how we assess. To mark numerically, that is, out of 20 or 10 or whatever total, tells us very little about pupil performance. The mark $^{5}/_{10}$ says nothing about performance except that he or she is better than approximately 50 per cent and worse than 50 per cent. It does not describe what a pupil can do, but simply places them in rank order. After all, in a test with two questions both marked out of 10, a pupil may obtain $^{10}/_{20}$, a probable pass mark, in eleven different ways! It is far more informative to both pupil and teacher if a six- or four-point scale is used throughout the languages department, possibly in all years, for all assessment.

Each point on the scale is then carefully described in terms of pupil performance. A six-point scale can be applied to all written work, while a four-point scale is adequate for assessing oral work.

Below is an example of what is meant, adapted from both the criteria for the NEA assessment scheme and those produced by the Assessment of Performance Unit for their national assessment programme.

Written work can be assessed on the following scale:

1 – Very little or practically no information relevant to the task is conveyed.

2 – Some relevant information conveyed with important omissions; very inaccurate and very little structure. Possibly incomplete sentences and may resort to English.

3 – Some relevant information conveyed, but structures basic and limited. Generally inaccurate.

4 – Conveys at least half of the relevant information using structured sentences, but which contain a number of inaccuracies.

5 – Conveys all or practically all of the information required in structured sentences which are generally accurate but contain some errors. Vocabulary adequate to the task.

6 – Conveys all or practically all of the relevant information using structured sentences which are generally accurate throughout. Shows a good range of appropriate vocabularly and the ability to go beyond a basic response.

Oral work can be assessed on the following scale:

1 – Pronunciation, use of vocabulary and fluency is such that very limited or virtually no communication takes place.

2 – Some response to the task with limited communication and exchange of information, which may be in incomplete sentences and with a possible resort to English.

3 – Responds quite well to the task and although there are mistakes in pronunciation and accuracy together with some hesitancy, this does not interfere with the basic communication of all or most of the message.

4 – Responds well to the task. Pronunciation and accuracy are generally good. There is a fluency of utterance and all or most of the information is conveyed using appropriate expressions. Shows ability to take initiative where required and to go beyond a basic response.

These are suggestions, and departments could rewrite definitions as they felt appropriate, but this style of marking is quicker, more accurate in assessing pupil performance and more informative than marking, say, out of 10. Certainly these are judgements and they may not always be as 'objective' as underlining and counting up errors, but there are two important considerations. Firstly, marking and counting up errors is negative, whereas the above gives credit for performance and emphasises positive assessment. Secondly, teachers are professionals and should be perfectly capable of taking responsibility for the assessment of their pupils' performance; judgements are made in the light of professional expertise and experience, and teachers do not need to count grammatical errors or to rank children in order to make accurate statements about pupils' attainment.

It is also worth noting that the above scheme is relatively simple but, in a positive system of assessment, the degree of success is easier to state than that of failure in a negative system. With an emphasis on speaking, and the use of group and pair-work in the classroom, the above system makes oral assessment much easier, since two or more pupils can be assessed at the same time.

4 A new approach

THE SYLLABUS

The scheme of work is probably the most important document produced by a department, since it should be the definitive statement of the rationale governing the teaching of languages within a school. The contents will cover all aspects of the subject area, but the core is the description of the teaching programme – the syllabus. Examinations have always affected the content of the teaching programme, usually adversely, but it must be emphasised that there is a great difference between a testing and a teaching syllabus. The former should come out of the latter; the testing syllabus states the parameters of the examination, while the teaching syllabus should aim to go further and extend all pupils according to their ability. The way in which the language to be taught is set out and then presented in the classroom is all-important, since this will affect the interest, and hence the motivation, of the learner. In the fourth and fifth years, every unit of language taught ought to have an end product – the learner is required *to do something* with what he or she has learnt; it must be clear that there is a purpose to what is being presented and taught, so that the completion of the task becomes important and the language is then the vehicle for carrying out the task.

The advent of GCSE has caused departments to examine carefully their syllabuses, and the effect of this will be beneficial in many ways for languages in the curriculum. However, some dangers are becoming obvious. This chapter sets out an approach to the teaching programme which will hopefully help teachers to avoid certain pitfalls. As previously stated, one of the most positive developments in GCSE is the precise nature in which the testing syllabus is set out. Topic areas, settings, vocabularly and structures are clearly stated at basic and higher levels, while the national criteria set clear guidelines for text and test-types. The teacher knows exactly where he or she stands with respect to the examination. However, a teaching syllabus described in these terms limits both the language presented and the activities in the classroom. The tendency has been for departments to rewrite their schemes of work according to the topic areas required, and to set these out, together with vocabulary and structures, at both basic and higher levels. It might typically look like Figure 1.

While on the one hand this gives a clear indication of what the teacher is required to present, on the other it raises two problems. Firstly, language acquisition does not take place in discrete topic areas, any more than in discrete skills. While it is quite possible *to test* in discrete skill areas within specific topics, e.g. reading signs, menus or notices, it does not make for good

▼ *Fig. 1 Scheme of work for a topic area*

Topic: Daily routine				
Basic level				
Setting	*Function*	*Structures*	*Task*	*Materials*
Extended level				

practice to present language in this way in the classroom. Language should be presented in mixed skill and mixed topic situations, so that the learner is required to listen and respond by speaking or writing in situations which may cover several topics. A teaching syllabus written in this fashion may lead to a programme stating: weeks 1–2 daily routine, weeks 3–4 weather, weeks 5–6 transport, weeks 7–8 food and drink etc., so that topics are presented separately and with no obvious link between them. This is an exaggeration, but the tendency is already there.

If we examine carefully the topics required by the different consortia, it becomes evident that most of the topic areas and much of the vocabulary has been covered by the end of the third year. Indeed, many graded tests at level 2 show a similar degree of linguistic attainment to that of the core elements of basic-level GCSE. This gives rise to the second problem. How is teaching a language to be sustained over the last two years of a five-year course in an interesting, relevant and appropriate fashion? If teaching is carried out in discrete topic areas, is there sufficient appropriate material to maintain interest, avoid boring repetition and to introduce new elements? These are problems which have already made themselves manifest, particularly with pupils who are aiming at the basic grades, and may lead to some of the work done in fourth-year classrooms, with these pupils being no more advanced or demanding than that done in the second year. It is obviously demotivating when pupils can see no evident progress or purpose in their learning.

Thus it becomes essential that the scheme of work presents the teaching programme in years 4 and 5 in such a way that the complete syllabus for GCSE is adequately covered. The teaching situations and tasks have to be such that the pupil is actively involved and extended. If there is an end product, language is acquired in a meaningful way. One possible solution is for the teaching programme in the fourth and fifth years to be presented in large units of work, two to three a term. This would, in effect, be project work, with pupils required to accomplish a number of tasks leading to the presentation of a project which, for productive work, could include taped and written language and wall displays or folders, while having required a great deal of reading and listening in order to elicit information. All necessary grammar or structures would have been worked into the programme by the teacher and a range of topic areas covered. There would have been a purpose for this language, i.e. the completion of the project or end product, and pupils could work at different levels according to their ability. This end product would also be easily assessable, and therefore continuous assessment or profiling would be relatively easy to accomplish.

An example of this might be the production by each pupil of a large wall display on the detailed description of another member of the class. The pupils would be given basic information on a completely different character and then required to role-play that character, so that everyone would produce two separate detailed descriptions. These descriptions would have taped as well as written elements, e.g. a taped dialogue when each pair is finding and giving personal information. The topics covered would be daily routine, home, family, school, leisure activities, holidays and future plans, across a range of settings. The present and future tenses would be covered, as well as perfect and, in French, possibly the habitual use of the imperfect. Assuming that the perfect had been taught earlier, the teacher may well wish to present and teach this use of the imperfect and introduce the simple future, or just reinforce *aller* plus infinitive. In order to increase vocabulary, pupils could do a great deal of reading – descriptions from stories or poems – and listen to songs, or tapes with pupils from, for example, a twin school giving descriptions of their friends, teachers or parents. Thus a wide range of topics and settings could be covered, necessary grammar taught and all the four skills adequately practised. The able pupil could be extended by more advanced reading and listening materials, while every pupil could work at his or her own level. Most importantly, pupils could work with authentic materials in authentic or quasi-authentic situations and, since there is an end product, the language learnt and used would be purposeful.

Such an approach to a scheme of work or teaching programme might be set out as shown in Figures 2 and 3.

The second example, Young Enterprise Publicity Campaign, would allow pupils to work within the broad topic areas of town and work, with particular emphasis on descriptive and persuasive language. Reading matter would be mainly brochures and advertisements, and pupils would produce similar brochures on their own area, as well as *guides sonores et télévisés* with the aim of 'selling' their town to attract tourism or industry. In addition, they might take a product, perhaps even made in the school, such as soft toys or jewellery, and produce publicity to encourage a possible sale of these items to a twin school abroad. If the school is twinned with a French school, that could be their

▼ *Fig. 2 Example of a scheme of work*

Project: To produce large wall display giving personal descriptions of two people: (a) classmate (b) an older person

Time: Term 1, weeks 1–5

Activities	Topic areas	Settings	Notions/ Functions	Structures	Materials
Write list of questions Listen to taped dialogues (description) Give and seek, orally, personal information Read various descriptions Record taped information (make a tape) Write an account of a person Role-playing	Personal details Daily routine Home and family School and work routine Future plans Free-time and leisure interests Food and drink Health and welfare Holidays	Home and school Youth club Places of entertainment Sports centre etc.	Giving and seeking information Stating opinions and seeking others Expressing likes and dislikes Stating intentions Stating and finding out what people can do Stating and discussing interests	Question forms Adjectival agreement, superlatives Perfect Imperfect Simple future *aller* + infin. *venir de, en train de, sur le point de* Negatives Expressions of quantity Prepositions	

▼ *Fig. 3 Example of a scheme of work*

Project: Young Enterprise Publicity Campaign for (a) town, (b) product

Time: Term 3, weeks 6–10

Activities	Topic areas	Settings	Notions/ Functions	Structures	Materials
Reading brochures Writing brochures Discussing advertisements Tape-recording town descriptions Making a video advertising a product Role-playing Writing a questionnaire	Local environment Shopping Public Services Public transport Entertainments Money matters	Place of work Places of entertainment Town Shops Information office Bank Public transport	Giving and seeking information Getting things done Expressing want or desire Expressing preference Asking, inviting or directing others to do something	Question forms Adjectives a) agreement b) comparison Prepositional phrases Imperative Future Quantifiers Present tense Future tense Expressions of quantity	Town brochures and worksheets Advertisement from a) television b) magazines Department OHP Department text and worksheets

target. Again, a wide range of topics and settings is covered, a number of grammatical structures are used and all four skills are practised. The materials used are authentic and the language and tasks are appropriate, relevant and useful, while each learner can produce worthwhile work according to his or her own level of competence.

Another advantage of such an approach is that each end product, in its various elements, is assessable, either in discrete or in mixed skills. Marking could be done on a 0–3 or 0–5 basis for speaking, reading, listening and writing as appropriate.

What is shown here is offered as example only, and there may well be omissions within the various headings, but each department could adapt according to their own resources and ideas, changing or adding to the activities and materials as necessary.

THE SCHEME OF WORK

It is the function of the effective scheme of work to make what has hitherto been implicit within the syllabus explicit. It should therefore contain:

1 Details of how the department is organised, to take into account the language teaching programme in the school and the day-to-day routine organisation, lists of duties and responsibilities etc.
2 The aims and objectives of the department's language teaching. These objectives may well have to be differentiated according to the stage and ability of the pupils. One major advantage of the integrated skill approach which we advocated is that it allows for differentiation of task within a given group. The final product as well as the process will have to be assessed according to these differentiated objectives. This is yet another reason why each department must have formulated its teaching and assessment objectives explicitly. It is no longer acceptable for an individual teacher to use classroom practice and assessment methods which are founded on assumed, unexpressed objectives and criteria. These must be made clear to colleagues, pupils, parents and other interested parties.
3 A detailed account of teaching methods, resources and assessment. If communicative and integrated skills are to have high priority within the stated objectives, then the teaching strategies will have to reflect these objectives. Departments will need to itemise within their schemes of work how they use the target language, the type of resources, teacher attitude towards error, differentiated tasks, authentic materials, discrete and integrated skill assessment, etc.

At the same time, departments must develop the means to evaluate their success in achieving these objectives. They will need to suggest a procedure whereby the efficacy of the objectives and the performance of both teachers and learners are evaluated. More detailed information about the organisational aspects of teaching foreign languages is contained in the NALA publications *Foreign Languages in Schools*, *Self-Evaluation of Foreign Language Departments* and *Producing a Scheme of Work.*

Implementing the objectives

Having considered the implications of the introduction of GCSE for the department in broad terms, it is now left to the teacher to implement departmental objectives within the classroom. The broad syllabus stipulates certain modules providing the framework for teaching over a period of time, and which make for purposeful language use. We shall deal in later chapters with the most appropriate methodology and resourcing for such an approach but, again, it is important the teachers in the department produce agreed guidelines and a common policy. Until now, the implementation of a communicative approach within the classroom has been hindered because teachers have confused teaching with the testing syllabus. We have shown how the advent of the graded test movement, though positive in its intentions, sometimes produced in classrooms the substitution of topics and their associated vocabulary for the grammatical structure and lexis of the traditional course without the requisite change in methodology. There is a danger that the GCSE syllabus will suffer the same fate, unless modern language teachers grasp the nettle of making *methodology* more communicative as well as *content*.

It is, therefore, essential that the syllabus produced by a group of teachers for the purpose of preparing pupils for the GCSE examination should distinguish very carefully between 'input' and 'output' aspects. The 'input' we have suggested is the teaching syllabus which provides modules of wider language use subdivided into differentiated tasks. These tasks are appropriate to the ability of the pupils, the methodology and resources to be exploited and the length of time available for each lesson. The syllabus designer has to ensure that all the topics and settings prescribed by the chosen examination consortium are covered by the tasks or modules. This is not the same as starting from the prescribed list in order to create a programme. The end result might be similar, but the emphasis and purpose has been to create a course which might stimulate the interest of the pupils and encourage them to communicate because they wish to. This means that every module and task listed in the scheme of work must contain:

1 Activities and texts (of a varied and authentic nature) designed to develop creative language behaviour.
2 Clearly formulated aims and objectives, means of assessing pupils' success and evaluating the process.
3 Guidelines for the teacher as to how the topics materials are to be exploited for communicative language use.

The output is a list of the intended learning outcomes which the pupil is required to master during the course, module or task. Within this syllabus is contained explicit information on the skills, both integrated and discrete, which the learner will be expected to control by the end of a given unit. The syllabus designer must again ensure that these learning outcomes are compatible with the GCSE examination requirements but not necessarily a mirror-image of them, since language used purposefully will go beyond the limitations of a mere examination syllabus. The classroom teacher must not present the list of topics and settings it contains as a series of structures to be learned by heart or vocabulary to be tested by a recall test. Although both these activities may be a component of a pre-communicative teaching programme, they do not constitute a valid objective or learning outcome in their own right.

Language and communication

It is still important that pupils should consciously exploit language in a variety of situations and not limit themselves to a regurgitation of pre-learnt structures. Language should not be regarded as the sum total of its discrete elements. There is a need to apply the linguistic forms acquired during one activity to the different requirements of another. Since teaching is a conscious activity and the classroom, of necessity, an artificial environment, this transfer of acquired forms must be a more or less conscious process. We can never hope to equip our pupils with every imaginable linguistic variation to be produced at wish with absolute accuracy from the recesses of their retrieval system. We can, however, equip them with the confidence and experience that teaches them to adapt a structure or substitute a synonym should the need arise in a given situation. This process has an infinite number of variables contained within it: from the conscious teaching of a grammatical structure at the one extreme, to the provision of a loose linguistic paraphrase at the other. The mere fact that our ultimate goal is communicative language teaching and learning does not absolve us from the responsibility of providing the order and coherence of that process.

The introduction of a course designed to facilitate communication within the classroom requires, within the scheme of work, the formulation and also consideration of the following areas:

1 **Methodology.** It would be counterproductive to evolve a course, module or task whose aim is primarily communicative and not consider the implications for methodology. We shall discuss these in detail in a later chapter. It is obvious, however, that the foreign language is to be used in the classroom as the primary communicative agent and event. The teacher must develop strategies that encourage this use – such as simulation and games – and should not intrude into the flow of the resultant communication with overzealous attention to error correction or structure learning.

2 **Resources.** Apart from the normal coursebook supplemented with material presented on the tape recorder, the teacher will have to equip the classroom with a battery of realia, presentation equipment, authentic texts – written, audio or video – and finally props which help to maintain the flow of communicative activity in a given situation. Again, we shall detail these requirements in a later chapter.

3 **Teacher training.** Time must be allocated in order to train teachers of modern languages the communicative use of language in the classroom and strategies to promote it. Since the introduction of GCSE calls for an adjustment in methodology for many trained teachers, an equivalent in-service training programme will have to be organised with the same purpose in mind. The LEA, through its advisory body, may take initiatives in this direction. However, the Head of Department must be prepared to accept responsibility for leading a programme of training within the department. The scheme of work will contain an outline of this programme which could contain a reformulation of classroom interaction, strategies for developing communicative activity, positive assessment of the language skills demonstrated and evaluation of the processes involved.

4 **Assessment.** Teachers of modern languages will have to differentiate accurately in their assesment of pupil performance, between the various language skills and between the various objectives set for pupils at different levels of ability. Their assessment and reporting will have to reflect this differentiation and provide the information required for an examination entry pattern which has 24 variables. The resulting assessment profile will, of necessity, reflect performance in a highly differentiated manner since the final examination will asse. performance on a *single* continuum rather than the traditional GCE/CSE *double* continuum with overlap of grades. This will mean that a global assessment based on traditional criteria, in which written and spoken accuracy are paramount, will give way to a broader but more precise assessment of communication in all four skills. Both student and practising teachers will have to be trained in alternative assessment techniques which do not necessarily rely on the class or individual test to assess performance in individual skills. It may be more appropriate to assess performance as part of the communicative classroom process, particularly in the case of an oral assessment, which all teachers recognise to be time-consuming for both pupils and teachers.

In order to justify examination entry at a particular level, teachers will have to provide evidence of performance which differentiates clearly between the target skills which have been listed as objectives for the course leading to GCSE. It may be limited to a graded performance in the four language areas identified, but might wish to take into account other assessment objectives such as pronunciation, fluency, ability to process information, control of idiom, ability to manipulate structure, ability to carry out instructions in the foreign language, etc.

OVERVIEW

The creation of a course leading to GCSE which exploits an integrated and purposeful use of the language will clearly influence teachers of modern languages. A syllabus which tackles language in terms of topics and settings, notions and functions cannot be approached in an identical fashion to a syllabus which uses grammatical structure and thematic vocabularly as its base. We have outlined ways in which an integrated but topic-based approach can be broadened into wider units or modules in order to create a purpose behind the communicative language. This will avoid repetition of material and methodology used at the elementary stages of language learning and will obviously influence language work carried out up to and post-GCSE. An integrated approach based on authentic materials, topics and settings cannot be sprung upon unsuspecting pupils in the two years prior to GCSE. They will have to be well prepared in terms of both methodology and materials from the very start of their course. Neither is it beneficial to expect them to abandon these valid objectives when they continue to a more advanced level. Universities and examination boards are already re-evaluating their own assessment patterns and criteria in order to align themselves and their examinations with the demand for a more communicative and functional approach to language.

There may be some teachers who will claim that the approach we have suggested will not work with their pupils for reasons of timetabling, resources, personalities and a host of equally burdensome difficulties. We believe that the advantages it offers will provide the impetus to overcome the difficulties which may, at first sight, appear great. This approach:

- avoids repetition of material and methodology, thus preventing pupil boredom
- creates situations to use language with a purpose
- will appeal directly to pupils' interest and thus improve motivation
- is an integrated-skill approach which allows the teaching of modern languages to compare more readily with the areas of experience advocated by the HMI document, *Curriculum 5–16*
- builds on previous work undertaken in the language teaching programme
- has an end-product readily assessable at different levels of linguistic competence and with various target objectives. This will fit easily within the DES demand for a profiled record of achievement.

- allows pupils to perform at their own level of competence in individual skills, although an element of 'guided' selection of activity will have to be maintained by the teacher to ensure pupil progress.

In later chapters we shall discuss how the programme we have advocated is to be translated into classroom practice in terms of activities, methodology and materials. Most teachers will be able to take these suggestions and adapt them for their own purposes; others will use them as a basis for their own teaching programme. It is important that teachers do not regard each lesson as a didactic unit but plan a series of lessons around a single module and that the activity and approach are varied to stimulate pupils' interest.

5 Implications for the classroom

AIMS AND REQUIREMENTS

The seven primary aims set out in the *National Criteria* are those which every teacher of modern languages should seek to pursue in setting up a course leading to the examination at GCSE. Language teachers should address the question of whether their methodology:

- develops the ability to use language effectively
- forms the sound base of the skills for further study
- offers insights into the culture and civilisation of the target language
- develops an awareness of the language
- provides enjoyment and intellectual stimulation
- encourages positive and sympathetic attitudes to foreign cultures and languages
- promotes learning skills of a more general application.

We have already discussed how the course designer might usefully work towards these ends and fulfil the demands set out above; it is now left to the classroom teacher to make sure that his or her methodology, use of materials and classroom activities also reflect these ideals in the various skill areas.

To be effective within a course leading to GCSE, activities must conform to the following requirements:

1 They must be taught with full integration of all language skills. It would be artificial to isolate one skill because it happens to suit the teacher's assessment requirements. Genuine communication demands we use all language modes. Certain activites will inevitably emphasise one or more skills over others, but this should not influence our overall strategy for integrated language. Assessment should, where possible, become part of the process, but may still require a discrete skill approach. GCSE certainly treats the language in this way.

2 Activities may be used as a single component of the modules we have suggested or, alternatively, as a mini-module in their own right if they fulfil the primary requirement above. For example, an activity can include information which is extracted from a taped source, communicated to a group, who then process it into another form or solve a problem and then record or present that material – as visualised in Figure 1. This model acts as a paradigm for many classroom activities and can be enlarged into a full module

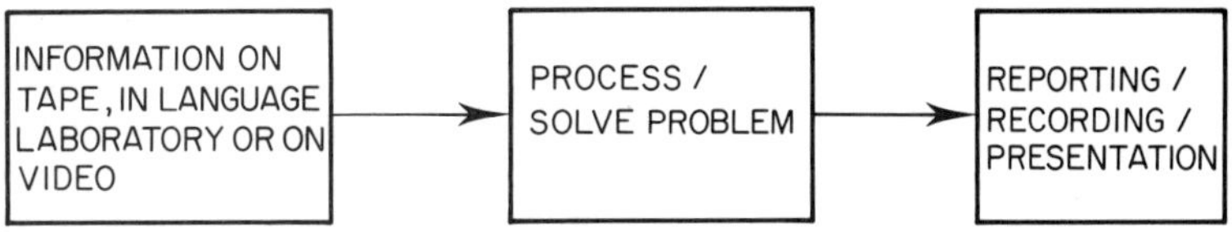

▲ *Fig. 1 Model of information-processing activity*

incorporating all skills and a variety of the topics and settings of the GCSE syllabus.

3 Activities must, at least in part, provide opportunities for pupils to meet and use the requisite settings and topics for GCSE within the appropriate skill areas. The modern languages department will have designed a scheme of work which incorporate these. It is left to the individual classroom teacher to ensure that this is translated into classroom practice using authentic resources and communicative strategies.

COMMUNICATIVE STRATEGIES

If the products of a language course geared towards the traditional external examination were unable to cope when faced with the demands of the real world and communicating with a native speaker or an authentic text, how is the teacher to structure the classroom activity so that the pupils show more confidence in such a situation? The answer is to move away from the study of language for its own sake and towards encouraging pupils to communicate in a medium that happens to be a foreign language. Krashen has shown that, for genuine language acquisition to take place, the pupil's attention must be focused away from a study of linguistic form and towards the transmission of relevant information. In doing so, we direct them towards a genuine purpose for communication. It follows from this requirement that the activity should stimulate the pupil's interest in its own right. If we merely concentrate on the *learning* of a linguistic structure or topic (to borrow Krashen's distinction) this will influence but cannot control the *acquisition* of that language. By directing the pupils towards a study of the medium we run the risk of disinterest and disaffection among our clientele, as the pattern of pupil choice in fourth year option schemes tends to illustrate. Pupil attitude is as important as aptitude, and by directing them towards an interesting message, we are more likely to motivate them and to stimulate communication.

The most effective second-language users are those who can apply a pre-learnt structure to a natural communicative situation without interfering with that flow of communication. Too much emphasis by the teacher on the correctness of the utterance will deflect from the need to communicate. We must ensure no carefully compiled and resourced classroom activity can be carried out successfully by the pupils without the necessary tools to complete that activity. Littlewood's distinction between communicative and pre-communicative activities holds good.

Once these principles have been established, the classroom strategies and activities will flow from them. Many may appear at first sight to bear close resemblance to the grammatical or audio-lingual activities which they replace. They will, for instance, frequently involve question-and-answer techniques. This basic technique contains within it an infinite number of learning intentions which will vary with the type of activity, the target skill, the level and finally the interest of the pupil.

Teachers are adept at ringing the changes on the type of questioning which relates to a particular linguistic goal. Thus, a teacher using a particular picture might ask: *Womit spielen diese Jungen*? or *Was hat das Mädchen eben getan*? The activity might be nominally communicative, but every teacher of German will recognise that in the first example the target structure to be elicited is the noun in the dative case and in the second example the verb in the perfect tense. Even when appealing to the pupil's own interests and personal experiences the target very often remains the 'learning' of a linguistic structure or a area of vocabularly. There is no harm in this; indeed, it remains a valid exercise, provided the teachers are aware that the methodology they are using is aimed primarily at the tools for linguistic insight rather than a genuine stimulus for communication. It is therefore quite acceptable for such questioning to be used in listening, speaking, reading and writing activities. However, the activity will only be 'owned' by the pupil and motivation increased if there is a *real* reason to communicate as far as that can be contrived within the confines of the classroom.

In order to illustrate this distinction further, let us consider how the same language outcome might result from divergent linguistic intentions. Asking *Wo liegt mein Buch*? is a communicative activity leading to possible language acquisition if the questioner genuinely does not know the whereabouts of his or her book. Immediately, there is a perceived need to communicate resulting from a simple information gap. The impulse to answer comes from the wish to communicate and not an acquiescence to a linguistic task imposed by the teacher.

What happens if the same question is repeated with the book in question lying in front of the teacher who is frantically pointing at it? Then the activity, with its perceptible artificiality, becomes a learning exercise with a specifically structured outcome. As such, it may, indeed, have its place as a 'pre-communicative' or 'monitor learning' activity, but the teacher must be aware of this fundamental distinction and plan the activity accordingly.

It is no coincidence that various books on language teaching techniques concentrate on the early stages of language acquisition and learning for their examples, for it is at this stage that real acquisition is at its most intense and what Krashen refers to as the 'affective filter' is at its lowest. Teachers of first- or second-year beginners will be familiar with the following features: high motivation, positive orientation to this as yet novel form of communication, low anxiety with regard to error and a high degree of acquired self-confidence in at least oral and aural skills. Teachers are aware, too, of the problems of sustaining this positive attitude throughout a four- or five-year examination course where the demands of the examination have meant that the methodology adjusts to the learning and study aspects of the language. The introduction of the GCSE will not represent a total panacea for this problem, since it inevitably retains the anxiety created by the need to assess pupils in discrete language skills at a dictated point of time.

However, the requirements of the national criteria and the change of emphasis from accuracy to communication in the assessment criteria of all examination consortia provide language teachers with an opportunity to alter their methodology. If genuine communication is an assessment objective for our examination syllabus, then our classroom practice should reflect this. We have suggested in the previous chapter that our course or scheme of work should not necessarily reflect in mirror-fashion the topics and settings of our examination syllabus, since this is not always the most stimulating approach for communicative teaching. It may be more acceptable to teach around modules which contain the requisite topic area, morphology, syntax and situations demanded by the GCSE examination. Such modules are more likely to appeal to the pupils' interest, since they can be designed to relate to their imagination or field of experience. We have also suggested that, although the final GCSE assessment targets discrete skills, a communicative approach demands mixed-skill teaching based on authentic materials wherever possible. The arrival of coursework and criterion-referenced assessment will then present few problems to teachers using this approach.

The proposals we set out in that chapter do not provide a complete course leading to GCSE; they merely put forward certain principles and approaches upon which the teacher may base their classroom practice.

COMMUNICATION TECHNIQUES

Interpersonal communication falls into four main categories:

1 talking about oneself;
2 talking about an object or topic of interest;
3 talking about human contact or relationships;
4 expressing a need for something or a prohibition.

Given that people speak or write in these main areas of interest, it is then necessary to decide how best to elicit communication so that it does not remain a language-practising exercise but a purposeful and meaningful act of communication. The following techniques are the most suitable for stimulating communicative activity among pupils and the most likely to encourage them to speak or write:

1 information-gap techniques;
2 conveying personal information and experiences;
3 problem-solving techniques;
4 imagination-stimulating techniques and role-play;
5 games;
6 opinions and issues (post GCSE).

In each of these activity types the attention is consciously shifted away from the 'problem' of language and towards an activity which requires language in order to function. The teacher will select from one of these activity-types, or may prefer a mixture of two or more, in order to stimulate language with a particular purpose. The early stages of language acquisition will rely on a mixture of pre-communicative structure and vocabulary building and the more communicative activities we have listed above. Our concern is here with the course leading to GCSE, but the approach will clearly have implications for both the elementary and post-GCSE stages, and we shall consider these later. It would be inappropriate for the teacher, in the later stages of a language course leading to GCSE, to launch into a mixed-skill, language-with-a-purpose teaching technique if the pupils have not been previously well prepared for such an approach. In practical terms, the teacher would then have to incorporate some of the topics and settings common to most GCSE syllabuses into the earlier stages of his or her course. Indeed, which commercially-produced course does not include in its preliminary stages topics such as personal identification, school, travel, shopping, food and drink, and geographical surroundings?

1 Information-gap techniques

We have suggested that one of the most fundamental activities which is readily adaptable for classroom purposes is the information-gap technique whereby one pupil or group of pupils is in possession of information which others have the task of eliciting. The method commonly used in the traditional classroom is that of the teacher having the information and needing to transfer that linguistic information to the pupils. This, indeed, is the fundamental flaw in so much traditional classroom interaction: the teacher has the difficult task of drawing pupils' interest closer to the language he or she is hoping to transfer to the pupil. This process may be represented as in Figure 2.

It is the teacher's aim in this model to familiarise pupils with the structure of language. It is left to the expertise of the teacher, the appropriateness of the materials and the efficacy of the methodology and classroom activities to judge how far along our

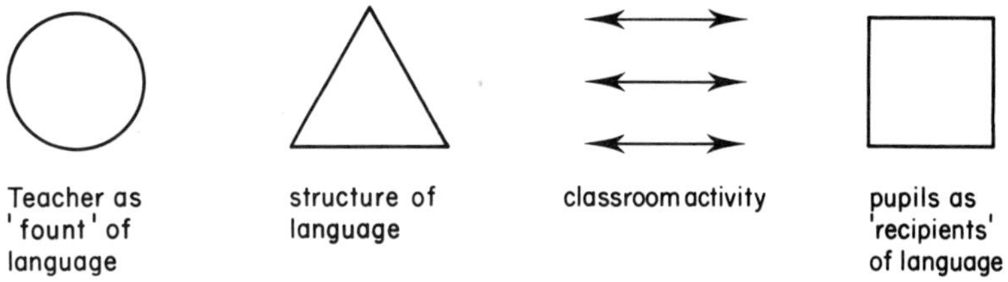

▲ *Fig. 2 In the traditional classroom*

linear tramlines the teacher has pushed the body of language he or she is seeking to transfer.

Whatever techniques the teacher may use within the classroom, the intention is always to effect the convergence of the pupil interest and the study of language. The teacher is both the source and the controller of language activity. The more effective teachers will, of course, exploit pupil interest by using more pupil-centred communicative activities and, in so doing, draw the pupils closer to the target language. However, because he or she has to juggle the dual roles, the teacher's position remains at best demanding and at worst untenable.

If we recompose the same components of classroom interaction so that we base our strategy firmly on pupil interest and experience, constructing activities which use language in order to communicate, then the whole becomes a purposeful language activity

with the teacher as an all-pervasive 'enabler'. This may be visualised as in Figure 3. The advantage of this model is that pupils cannot escape from the medium of language; it is no longer something which the better motivated will accept and the less motivated reject – which was frequently possible with the linear model. This activity depends for its very survival on the target language.

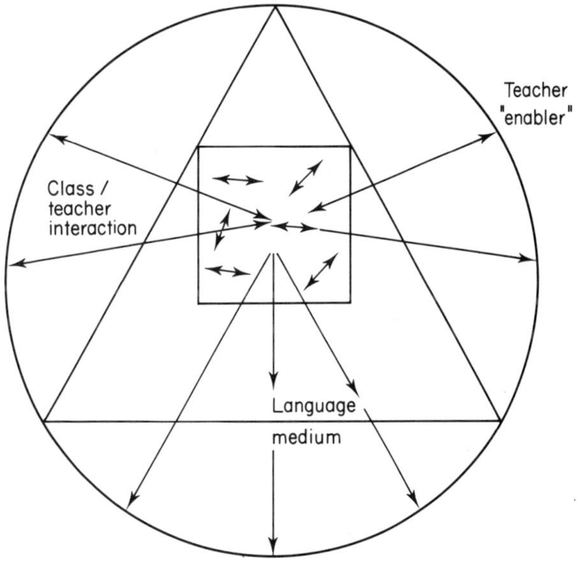

▲ *Fig. 3 In the GCSE-oriented classroom*

How, then, will these principles translate themselves into GCSE classroom practice? When we have constructed in the classroom an information gap, questions must be asked by pupils and teachers in order to overcome that gap. It should be remembered throughout what we have to say about information-gap techniques that the teacher is now no longer the sole controller and arbiter of the classroom activity. The pupils' interest will now play a central part. The criteria for success are also altered: it is the bridging of the information gap rather than the production of correct language which signals the success of the performance.

It is still left to the teacher to construct, maintain and evaluate that activity. We shall make various suggestions under each category heading; the teacher must adapt these suggested activities to the requirements of the individual class group and the language module being undertaken within that class. Thus, the suggested activities should in no way be seen as prescriptive or complete in themselves – they are merely activity types which do not fall into any single category but reveal features of all of them.

(a) Information gap using personal details

This will involve pupils finding out from each other and/or the teacher information based on personal details and experiences. It has several advantages: it is immediately motivating, since most people enjoy talking or writing about themselves; it provides an almost infinite resource bank if imaginatively exploited; it lends itself to variable approaches and levels. Finally, it is a fundamental communication activity applicable to real life.

The following are examples of such activites:

i 'Hot Seat'/'Heisser Stuhl'/'Chaise Chaude' etc: a short activity whereby a member of the class may be questioned by a partner, group or whole class on a given topic. It can be used as a part of a wider module, an independent revision activity or practice, or test for a linguistic topic.

ii Questionnaire-completing involving a general or specific topic – can be adapted from beginners to advanced level if resourced imaginatively.

iii 'Common denominator' exercises whereby pupils or groups question each other until they discover a common interest, like, dislike, leisure activity, aspect of home life, favourite drink, past experience, etc. As soon as they have discovered the common denominator, they move on to another pupil and repeat the process of mutual questioning. The teacher should decide how the results are recorded.

iv Interview techniques in order to elicit specific information. This may be used as a wider, statistic-gathering exercise, the results of which may be presented visually, verbally or in a combination of both. The teacher may be part of the activity, moving among groups to provide vocabulary, assess performance and to evaluate process.

As mentioned above, these information-gap activities may be seen as activities in their own right or a component or precursor to a wider module. For instance, the information gathered by means of interviewing members of the class might be presented statistically. The level may be adjusted, from bare personal details at beginners' level, to preferences, likes and dislikes at intermediate level to opinions and topical issues at advanced level. Another variation which again extends the potential is for participants to take on a persona rather than answering personally. We shall refer back to this extension under another section.

(b) Information gap using pictures and drawings

This techniques has a wide range of applications and the same advantage of the section above in that it may be exploited at both beginners' and advanced level, depending on the needs and abilities of the pupils. A picture in itself does not provide vocabulary and structures; it merely provides a stimulus to which pupils or teachers bring their linguistic and personal experiences which may be fruitfully interwoven with the elements of the picture to provide a linguistic context. The information-gap element is introduced by limiting what one pupil or group of pupils may see, exploiting the visual stimulus or introducing a variant.

i One pupil or a group of pupils questions another as to the content of the picture they cannot see. The final result may be a verbal/written or drawn reproduction in the case of a simple line drawing or a more advanced character portrait in the case of a photograph. The teacher may wish the group to decide on a group or pair description as a follow-up activity. The final product may then be compared with the original.

ii A carefully selected picture might provide a stimulus for a 'What has just happened? What is going to happen?' pattern of questioning. Picture series might also be approached in this way and divided into individual 'frozen' moments in time and exploited for their linguistic potential. This may not be a real-life situation but it is an authentically communicative one, if handled imaginatively. We shall explore this distinction a little later. The final product of the divided picture series might be a reconstitution of the pictures or merely a verbal discussion of the various incidents portrayed, possibly with pupils' suggestions and opinions.

iii 'Memory' and 'spot the difference' activities using pictures. These clearly belong in the games section but, as such, may be exploited as a testing of vocabularly and morphology in a more relaxed atmosphere. The techniques mean removing the picture in the case of memory suggestion and encouraging verbal participation in the 'spot the difference' type. An element of class competition may be introduced here, or the teacher may prefer to rely on pairwork or group co-operation in order to arrive at an agreed statement to be produced verbally or in writing.

(c) Information gap using television, video and computer

At first sight, there are many similarities with the activities listed above in that they are, at least partially, reliant on the visual image as a stimulus.

i The moving television/video image may be exploited as we have exploited the pictures above, with the advantage that the more real-life element of the moving image can introduce a more natural use of tenses than the static image allows. The sound element may or may not be appropriate for the level of the group. If it is inappropriate, then the teacher should not be afraid of using the volume control button to 'speak over', commentate or explain the dialogue. The pause and re-wind facilities are useful for 'freezing' and repetition.

ii To eliminate the problem of 'TV glaze' associated with pupils watching their favourite medium, teachers should ensure that pupil involvement and communication are switched on by introducing information-gap elements such as:

- the screen turned away from one section or group in order that others have to find out what has happened, is happening, is going to happen;
- skim and scan skills, which we shall elucidate when speaking about the use of written texts, being used to extract information from the programme;
- the volume turned down initially to use merely the visual element so that pupils can supply a dialogue or commentary.

iii One must distinguish between exploiting a video programme for its communicative potential and producing a video programme with a camera. This has enormous potential which we shall mention when we discuss imagination and role-play. These technical aspects within the classroom provide a rich source of relevant and communicative transactions in the foreign language.

iv Computers and computer programs are now increasingly adding to the language teacher's arsenal. In their early days, programs were produced on an isolated linguistic component, usually an element of lexis or grammar, introducing and practising it in a relatively unsophisticated way. Many teachers felt, quite justifiably, that they could carry out the same tasks more effectively themselves. They relied on these early programs for a fun or testing facility to be used for remedial or extension work. Computer programs in modern languages will probably retain this back-up function to work being carried out in the classroom. Recently, however, more sophisticated programs have been produced such as 'Granville'. These, if used imaginatively, can contribute to the communicative activity within the classroom by providing a resource bank in the foreign language and encouraging linguistic interaction of an integrated skill variety. Computers are still in their infancy in modern-language teaching, but they clearly have enormous potential within the modular integrated-skill approach we are advocating.

(d) Information-gap using tape recorders and the language laboratory

Although many language departments across the country are either dismantling language laboratories, or using them less and less, this is unfortunate. Language laboratories and their modern counterparts, the mini-labs, as well as tape-recorders, if used imaginatively, provide a potentially rich source of language activity within the communicative classroom.

i Tape-recorded material can be used as a source of information. This information may then be extracted by question-and-answer, text-searching or gist-understanding techniques, always remembering that it need not always be the teacher who controls these activities or the whole class which always participates at the same time. For example, one pupil from a group could be delegated, after discussion, to listen over the headphones of a language laboratory or cassette recorder to an aural message containing information which he then conveys to the group. He may need to return and write down a section he has missed or misunderstood. It is then the group's task to write down the simple message and present it orally or in writing to the rest of the class. This activity encourages listening, speaking and writing with a particular purpose and provides the information gap essential for meaningful communication. The teacher might increase the complexity of the task by inventing a simple verbal code in which the message is transmitted. This is then to be decoded by the remainder of the group.

ii Another approach may be to present the listening text as a source of certain information which must be transferred by individuals, pairs or groups into chart, graph, map, diary or statistical form. The advantage of this technique is that the purpose of the activity goes beyond the purely linguistic. It should therefore be assessed with that in mind; success will be measured against the criteria of the task itself: the extent to which pupils have achieved the transfer of material gleaned from the listening source and not a mere measurement of listening comprehension.

iii Listening with a purpose will be encouraged if pupils are asked to complete gaps left in a tapescript, or have to paraphrase what was said, again as a pair or group activity. Tasks become more communicative when they are performed co-operatively. There will always remain the danger of the intrusion of the mother tongue without ubiquitous teacher control. However, if the teacher remains consistent in his or her use of the target language, then pupils will be forced into a communicative listener's role, and the impact of the purpose of the message will become so much greater. Pupils may retain only a listener's role initially but, with time, they will accept naturally the need to play a more contributory part in the communication activity.

(e) Information-gap using written texts

The written form has traditionally provided the largest proportion of material for language work. This was reflected in the type and assessment of many examinations in modern languages. It will continue to provide a central position in material for the classroom, but GCSE requirements will mean that the nature of that written text will change from fictional language-specific material to 'authentic' material designed to convey a particular message. Some coursebooks are aware of this change and have altered the type of written work accordingly. This change of direction immediately creates the need for strategies for coping with an authentic text with a group that may not have the linguistic ability to assimilate it totally, while still being able to extract the message.

In the past, when a study of the language was the main objective, it was feasible to grade the semantic and syntactic level of the resource material according to both the requirements of the exercise and the linguistic level of the group. Indeed, the need for a sense of progression demanded this feature. Now that our attention has been diverted from the medium to message communication, there is an obvious need for authentic or stimulating messages to communicate. We shall deal at the end of this chapter with a definition of authenticity and a strategy for coping with such texts – both aural and written.

Written texts take the form of messages, signs, newspaper or magazine extracts, letters, statistical data, diaries, poems and short stories. With the last two, the objective is to stimulate the imagination rather than merely to convey a message. The pattern throughout the following suggested activities will remain the directing of pupils' attention to the content of the written stimulus.

i The first and most obvious type of activity based on an information gap with written stimulus is to provide one individual group with a timetable selection chart or menu from which they have to make a certain choice which must then be communicated to another group or individual. The results of this communication might be recorded in statistical or list form and presented on an OHP transparency or verbal presentation by a single member of the group.

Comprehension and communication will take place at

several stages. Firstly, there must be group discussion as part of the selection process. Then follows a communication of instructions to another group or individual and a means of ensuring that the message has been correctly transmitted and understood. Finally, the written or verbal presentation of results to the entire group may involve group reaction and discussion.

Let us consider a practical example of this broad technique. Teachers will be able to supply their own variations.

The class is divided into groups which are given the task of creating a programme for a hypothetical (or actual) visit to a foreign town, for which they have the necessary tourist information, town plan and entertainment guides. The idea is for each group to put foward a series of proposals. A spokesperson is sent from each group to become a member of a 'steering committee' which decides on an overall plan and allocates each group a task as a contribution to the final presentation. This could take the form of a wall poster, piece of prose, or series of OHP transparencies.

This activity could be seen as a single component of a larger module which includes writing for more information about the town and its surroundings, discovering its geographical location, comparing it with their own town, discussing travel and accommodation arrangements and presenting all of this prior to the visit. The urgency and motivation would, of course, be raised if the visit under scrutiny was real rather than hypothetical. The possibilites for follow-up activities after the visit are, of course, equally fruitful.

This activity is suggested as a component part of a larger 'Visit' module, but if one were to list the potential communication within that component, the list would be impressive:

- seeking and giving information
- discussing ideas
- problem-solving
- expressing reactions
- establishing and maintaining social relations
- giving instructions and conveying intentions

One could and should make a similar list with all communicative classroom activities, and include variations which will extend to other communicative possibilities such as acting out social roles, playing with language and talking one's way out of a problem situation. The stimulus might be any of those we have mentioned, from television to tape-recordings; the techniques and purposes might be many and varied, but the underlying intention remains the same: giving our pupils a reason to communicate meaningfully.

ii Posters and signs may be exploited in a similar but possibly less ambitious fashion, although in such cases the potential for communicative exploitation remains immense. On a factual level, information can be extracted and recorded or conveyed in another form. On a more imaginative plane, pupils could be encouraged into certain roles associated with these posters or signs. In order to do so they must not only comprehend the language but also use it in a meaningful manner.

Thus, faced with a poster advertising a travelling circus, a teacher could encourage groups of pupils to produce a tape-recording to be sent to a local radio station about the circus, or possibly interview the ringmaster for similar purposes. Another approach might be to produce a written report of a visit to that circus. Teachers know that, in order to perform such a task, pupils will be unable to avoid the use of past tenses. It would therefore be justifiable to spend time at this pre-communicative phase giving pupils the necessary skills to complete the task and teach the required forms. This should not be seen as a goal in its own right, but an ancillary skill which enables them to achieve their objectives more effectively.

The teacher using a reproduction of a sign outside the doctor's surgery might suggest the task of producing a daily diary for that doctor, which leads on to an activity involving a telephone conversation between a receptionist at the surgery and a patient who is suffering from stomach pains. An alternative approach might be for pairs of pupils to produce a tape-recorded interview between a reporter and the busy doctor in which she describes how she spends a typical day at home and the surgery.

iii An agony column or newspaper text may be reworked by changing the perspectives in which it is written. The father of the misunderstood daughter may be asked to respond in an interview or in a letter to the agony aunt. The newspaper article about sport hooliganism might be converted to an eye-witness account or police questioning of a participant. This technique will always require pre-communicative comprehension of the stimulus material followed by the active use of the language.

Observations on the use of information-gap techniques

These activities are communicative in the technical sense, although falling short of the purist's definition of a flexible and spontaneous communicative interaction. The classroom is an artificial environment, and the activities, of necessity, must be contrived. The more natural the teacher is able to make that linguistic environment, the less false the pupils will perceive the activity to be.

The teacher must be prepared to devolve responsibility for

the linguistic activity within the classroom. It need not always be the teacher who is asking the questions or controlling the role play. He or she may be more effective as the interviewee or the facilitator of linguistic situations generated by a group.

The information conveyed may appear in a variety of forms and should do so to avoid monotony of expectation.

The assessment of success must retain effectiveness of communication rather than accuracy of expression as its main criterion. There will always be a grey area where these two overlap, but the pupils' interest in the success of the activity is of paramount importance.

The information gap is the fundamental technique for encouraging communication, but it should not be regarded as a valid activity in isolation. Its most effective use is in conjunction with the other primary communication stimulators which we shall discuss. Indeed, each of them contains elements of the others, which is why an integrated approach is most likely to achieve success. Language is no longer broken down into its component parts but rather is seen as an entity.

2 Conveying information and experiences

This activity is a more specific aspect of the information-gap techniques we have just described and leads on from these information-gathering techniques. The judicious use of group or pair work will help to focus attention on the pupils' contributions as providers of linguistic activities, since these activites relate to them or their experiences, rather than to the teacher and the coursebook. Pupils may then be regarded as an essential and central resource for language work rather than the passive recipients of language from elsewhere.

We have listed suggested activities under this heading in the previous section, but we now look to methods for conveying the information and extending the activities we described. It was suggested there that the pupils' interest in themselves and their experiences would provide a rich source of activity material.

i Let us return to the 'common-denominator' activity where pupils have to discover something they have in common with other pupils in their class, such as interests, likes or dislikes, or something they had each done the evening before. A further extension at a more advanced level might be the introduction of a 'persona' – a favourite pop star, sporting personality, somebody they know well or can imagine by use of a photograph. Pupils are required either to assume the role of this person or to imagine likely characteristics. The extension of another persona has the advantage of broadening the base of experience and thus the linguistic potential of the situation. The teacher, however, must ensure that it does not trespass well beyond the pupils' capabilities and become an exercise in translation.

In suggesting an alternative persona to the pupils, or in

selecting anyone they know well for an information source, the teacher will help to ensure the activity will be more successful if there is an affective link – e.g. girlfriend, boyfriend/policeman/describing a thief/famous historical or contemporary figure/a favourite aunt/a disliked neighbour – all of whom are more likely to be more stimulating as an animator of communication. There is again a potential and fruitful overlap with all communication types: game element, drama techniques, information gap and the use of imagination.

The results might be recorded on a chart, bar graph, answers to a questionnaire or a short piece of prose in the form of a report. This introduces the skill of noting and recording information, and later transposing that information into another form – in itself a valid and valuable skill beyond the classroom.

ii Another extension of a common classroom activity in order to relate it more directly to the pupils' own interest is to produce a simplified map of the catchment area which can be combined with asking and giving directions in order to work out who lives where. This may then be converted into a game by pupils writing down the directions to their house on a piece of paper, the teacher or one of the pupils reading one out at random and the class having to guess to whom it refers.

iii Bus, train or air travel information can be presented in such a way that the information needs processing by the pupils in order to enable a specific activity to take place. These might be related to local requirements, thus awakening the personal interest of the pupils. The teacher may prefer to go for authenticity and use material in the target language.

The activity will appeal more directly to pupils' interests if they are given an individual or group task with the same timetable data. The teacher must take care that the authentic material does not present too many difficulties on its own without added linguistic concern. The skill of reading a continental timetable is an essential one which must be tackled prior to or as part of this activity.

Again, teachers will no doubt produce many imaginative variations in activity which will ensure that pupils' interests are awakened as they concentrate on the activities with a purpose. While the coursebook may be the source for much written material, it is important to vary the mode of presentation of pupils' work by making greater use of the walls and OHP transparencies in order to encourage movement and communication within the classroom. Immediately it will become less of a study and more of an authentic interaction.

3 Problem-solving techniques

This technique encourages pupils' communication by providing them with an external problem to solve requiring co-operation, discussion and thus language. The experience of mutal co-operation in order to overcome a difficulty will have the twin effect of improving pupils' confidence in the use of a foreign language to resolve difficulties and also to encourage positive negotiation and discussion between learners. Their belief in their own ability to process information, follow instructions, summarise material, arrive at conclusions and influence others in the foreign language will automatically be enhanced.

The problem to be solved must be within their capabilities and, preferably, close to their experience. We suggest that, at this level, it might involve familiar areas of experience such as travel and transport, maps, charts and timetables or stimulating and imaginative situations such as a detective or escape story. Again, each example we give should not be considered as a lesson in isolation but rather a part of a larger module moving towards the presentation of the final product. It is also likely that the examples will not be covered as a single lesson activity but a series of lessons. Teachers will have to adapt, adjust and amend any suggestions we make according to their own class requirements and introduce information-gap, role-play and game elements as appropriate.

i The class is given information about a planned visit to their town by pupils from a partner school abroad. It is their brief to prepare an information pack in the foreign language about their school, the town and its surroundings. This pack is to take the form of a brochure, an informative cassette-recording and a poster. The idea is to portray the subject matter in a lively and appealing form likely to interest the readers and listeners. Again, this might be a real or hypothetical situation, but is more likely to motivate the pupils if it is genuine. Every school has a potential recipient for such material in the form of a partner school or twinned town.

It is obviously an exercise which can only be attempted when the pupils' presentation and written production skills have reached a particular level, and it may need several practice runs earlier in their language course. It may also be enlarged to become a complete module involving an analysis of the school, community, local amenities, transport, history and geography, places of interest, and dubbed 'interviews' with locals. The very ambitious might want to produce a video as part of their presentation pack!

This activity and this type of approach has the advantage that pupils can make a valuable contribution at whatever their level of ability. If the correct groundwork has been carried out and pupils have been encouraged from an early stage to use the language they have acquired in a purposeful manner, then they will already have gained the necessary self-confidence in the foreign language to perform the tasks we have mentioned. The production of a school magazine or newsletter in the foreign language to send to the partner school might also be considered.

ii At a less ambitious level, but nevertheless using the same co-operation, discussion and problem-solving skills, the group or pairs can be presented with a picture or map and an associated problem to solve. The picture or photograph might show a person a group of people in a predicament, and it is the class responsibility to show how the predicament arose, what is happening and what the victims must do in order to escape their predicament. A picture of a car full of holidaymakers broken down at the roadside might be a familiar and possibly mundane occurrence. The same situation with a coach containing a football team which has broken down in an isolated spot might excite pupil imagination a little more.

The use of a map of a fictitious island or country containing a multitude of geographical obstacles and man-made traps might present a stimulating problem for a hypothetical group of prisoners escaping from the island. In both of these examples it is important for the teacher to present the problem in a manner that will both stimulate the pupils and introduce much of the language they will need in order to tackle the task. Imaginative use of visual and aural affects is therefore essential. One might even consider ways of rewarding the most effective solution to the problems posed.

iii It is also necessary to consider everyday problems that pupils might themselves encounter, as for instance, the planning of a party. Teachers should encourage groups to produce original ideas and good organisation. In the lead-in the teacher will familiarise his or her class with the requisite language and concepts, such as asking permission, sending invitations, planning games and activities, deciding on music and entertainment, preparation of food and drink, re-organising the furniture and controlling events on the evening. The final product of this classroom activity may be in written form, such as the design and wording of the invitation card. Pupils may prefer an aural presentation: a tape-recording of a typical telephone conversation between two teenagers discussing the party.

iv Another fertile area for teenager communication is comparing personality types. This may be linked with a problem-solving activity involving horoscopes, photographs (possibly taken from magazines, or borrowed from family albums) and character descriptions. The idea of this activity is to link certain people rather like a dating agency. Again, this is best performed in pairs or groups, since we are more concerned with the communicative process rather than the final product.

The first task is to establish a physical and personal description of the person they have selected. If it is someone in the class, they will have to interview them to establish these facts; if it is a television personality whose picture they have cut from a magazine, they will have to bring in a combination of creativity and fact-finding in order to build up a more complete profile. Having built up this profile, the next task is to present it, perhaps in the form of a series of posters around the classroom. It is then the task of groups or 'dating agencies' to effect certain combinations and justify their choice, perhaps even suggest forms of entertainment for the first meeting. A successful extension activity is reviewing and writing letters to the 'agony aunt' of a magazine, perhaps even the result of one such liaison set up by our dating-agency!

We have thus established the principles behind setting up a problem-solving activity and given examples which teachers might use in part or in entirety. It is important that pupils approach the problem without anxiety or fear of failure. We, the teachers, know that the communicative process is our primary concern; we wish, however, to instil a sense of enterprising spontaneity into our pupils with this type of activity. We should therefore set a tone of positive encouragement for their efforts, we must nurture our pupils' linguistic development, but we cannot allow negative assessment to dampen the fire of enthusiastic communication.

4 Creative and role-play activities

It is highly productive to stimulate the imagination of pupils. Acquiring a foreign language is providing them with an alternative means of communicating and, in so doing, providing them with an alternative perspective on life. This has a highly educational value, particularly at a stage in their lives when they are coming to terms with their own identity. 'Trying on' another persona adds a further dimension to this process.

In order to give the language we use in the classroom more meaning and context, we should provide the pupils with dramatic alternatives which they will enjoy experiencing. In so doing, we are breaking away from the idea that language can be studied in isolation and without a context. The *only* function of language is the context in which it appears. If you remove the context, you remove the reason for language. This is why we have concentrated on reasons for communicating. Drama techniques can be a vital means of providing that context without transporting the whole class to the foreign country and immersing them in that situation (which would also be contrived).

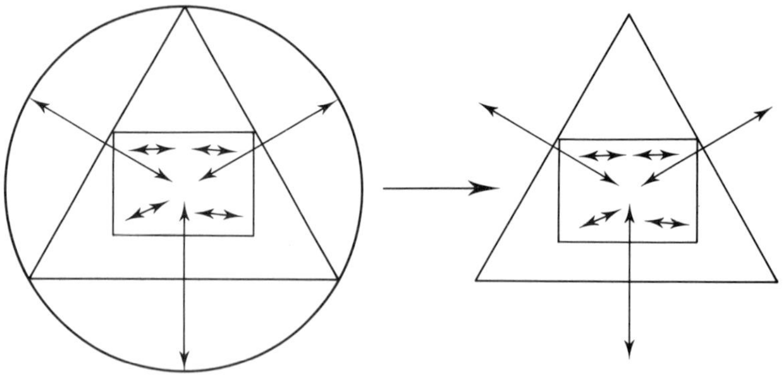

▲ *Fig. 4*

Another glance at our classroom communication model reveals how communication can still function, how the communicative activity is still viable, once the teacher control has been removed (Fig. 4). This would have been impossible in the traditional linear model of language study where language is treated in isolation. Any such transfer would have been merely fortuitous. Drama techniques therefore help to achieve the final phase of the development which takes the pupils from the precommunicative or input stage, through the controlled activity stage to spontaneous language use.

i Let us take as our starting point the standard role-play familiar to most teachers as part of the oral examination. It deals essentially with setting and structure, and is therefore frequently taught by giving the pupils a list of structures and vocabulary which they must learn and manipulate. Many teachers then attempt to provide pupils with a context and ask them to 'act it out'. Since the target is merely control of the structure and vocabulary, the performing activity can become repetitive and boring for the pupils. If, however, one concentrates on the setting, the role and the feelings of the participants in the role-play situation by, for instance, creating a conflict, then the standard role-play takes on an added meaningful dimension. Suddenly, instead of performing the linguistic gymnastics associated with a particular structure, pupils are communicating because they have something to say. For example, one can transform the standard situation at the station by making the porter rude and unhelpful, the grandmother anxious about meeting her grandson off a particular train, the businessman in a rush to catch a train which has already left, and a whole host of relevant and meaningful variations. All it requires is a stimulating input by the teacher in the form of a text, tape-recording, video, song, poster or scene enactment and a careful preparation of the roles.

ii An extension of this activity is the 'alibi' type situation where a crime has been committed and it is left to the various characters to create an alibi in order to establish their innocence. This might be as simple as an account of their actions between certain hours or as elaborate as linking with other characters in order to establish a common 'story'.

One extremely successful alibi situation involves creating a fictitious castle with a 'murdered' Count, and each of the many characters from the Countess, through the heirs to the Count's fortunes, to the maids, chauffeurs and gardeners all being given a motive to commit the crime. They have to establish their alibis, alone or in groups, before the 'interrogation', which is to be performed by a single detective (the teacher) and his panel of inquisitors (a group of pupils).

The teachers may not feel that establishing a guilty party is important, since we are concerned more with the questioning process than the outcome, but the pupils will certainly demand an outcome. One means of doing so is to give one of the characters a card with a cross on it. That character must then give one or two clues which might lead the inquisitors to the guilty party. A written report might then be required for police files.

iii Other useful role-play situations involve the use of telephone conversations, preferably performed with appropriate 'props' in a language laboratory, or simply sitting back-to-back. There are various ways of tackling this activity. One is to stimulate pupils' responses by providing them with a great deal of background information and suggesting the course the telephone conversation might take. Another is to provide very little information but add a constraint on each side. For instance, both want to go to a particular concert but know there is only one ticket between the two of them; or, in making an arrangement, one must be home by 7.30 p.m. and the other cannot leave until 7 p.m. A third possibility is to provide one half of the telephone conversation and allow the pupils to work in groups in order to produce the other half. The advantage of the telephone as a medium is that it forces pupils directly into an improved situation and ensures that they do not resort immediately to non-verbal communication. It also forces a dependence on the use of language in order to influence the direction of the conversation and to react to any unexpected course it might take.

iv Another specific area of exploiting drama techniques is the use of mime or dialogue in order to enact or complete a story. There is a wide range of possible input stimuli such as songs, magazine pictures, newspaper headlines, cartoons, picture series which have been split and need re-ordering, everyday objects in a strange context or combination such as a toothbrush and a torch. The activities which may emanate from such stimuli are again many and various. An obvious example is a simple description. That may be the final objective or merely a part-objective of a more ambitious activity, such as the production of a group story using the characters they have seen in a magazine photograph; or possible reasons for the strange combinations or contexts we mentioned above. The teacher might suggest a story which must include all such disparate articles or merely ask: 'What happened next ...?', when the pupils are faced with a cartoon or magazine photo or perhaps an outline of the story behind the newspaper headline. An interview with a television or sports personality might be the target activity if the pupils have been describing the photograph taken from a magazine. Here, the teacher is exploiting the pupils' own fund of information about such personalities, as well as retaining their interest in the subject matter. Such stimuli will naturally require support by the teacher in terms of vocabulary and structure, but these are included only in order to allow the activity to take place.

For example, if the activity is converted into a game and the stimulus is a mime by the teacher or group of pupils, then the teacher, by introducing the activity in the target language, and giving examples which have been discussed in the target language, will have provided much of the necessary linguistic material. If the pupils are motivated enough to want to express what they guess the mimed activity to be, and if the teacher has controlled their use of their mother tongue, then they will find a means of communicating their guess in the foreign language.

v At the post-GCSE level the teacher may continue the use of drama techniques within the classroom in order to stimulate effective communication. Students may be asked to play a particular role in the discussion of a social or political issue in order to broaden the base of the discussion and thus the linguistic potential. Again, the imposition of a particular stance in an issue of conflict always requires careful preparation and stimulating input, but the linguistic results are frequently more rewarding then a mere expression of personal opinion on a given issue. The teacher may wish to extend this role-play still further by imposing a situation involving inevitable conflict, such as the reason why one person or group should or should not receive a large amount of money, inherit a shipping empire, be the first group to colonise another planet, or the only group to survive an impending disaster. This type of activity may be structured as a debate, panel interview, written submission or open class forum.

These are just a few of the ways in which imagination might be stimulated and drama techniques exploited in order to provide situations for effective communication to take place. They share the common advantage of involving up to 30 pupils in an activity which requires language in order to function. The pupils then become a vital language resource for the teacher and serve simultaneously as language source and language target. The activity is more likely to succeed if the input is carefully selected and well resourced. We have mentioned before that the process is more important than the product from a communicative language teaching viewpoint, but the status of both might well be enhanced by recording the final product in writing, on a tape-recording or indeed a video-recording. It provides a further motivating factor and greater pupil pride in the final product.

5 Language games

Many of the activities we have described include a game or play element. They provide yet another means of sustaining pupil interest in an activity by making it enjoyable and the context meaningful. If our pupils are able to respond effectively to the context material, their acquisition of the necessary language is likely to be improved. Games also provide an effective means of breaking away from pupil and teacher interaction by providing contexts for pair and group work. They may include elements of all the other communicative activity types we have mentioned: information-gap, personal information, problem-solving and drama techniques.

We shall in this section suggest certain game types, give examples and allow the teacher to select the type and variety most appropriate to the language module in question. It must be stressed that games are to be seen as an integral part of language acquisition involving all skills rather than an alternative activity for light relief.

(a) Guessing games, question-and-answer games

These may be structured as a class, group or pair activity and involve the use of objects, pictures or other stimuli which one party has knowledge of and the other does not but has to find out. The purpose is to stimulate questioning activity by creating an information gap. At the simplest level, it might involve one half of the class guessing the home of an object or person which the other half cannot see. At a more sophisticated level, it might involve one person or group drawing a picture only another person can see, relying only on their description and the artist's questioning. This might provide an alternative approach to merely describing the picture, an activity familiar to many language teachers. One can force the questioning activity by insisting on only true/false or yes/no answers, or direct the questions towards the shape, size, colour, purpose and composition of the object.

(b) Picture, mime and sound games

In many respects these games are an extension of the previous category. Instead of objects or people to be described, we may use pictures, mime or sound in a similar way. A picture may be altered, a machine invented or an animal 'created' in order to stimulate discussion and description of the finished product. A mimed or sound source may be used in a similar fashion. It is easy enough to ask a pupil to record a series of everyday sounds such as babies crying, someone singing in the bath or a train passing, and then either use these as a guessing game or the stimulus for an imaginative story. Mime can be used in a similar fashion if pupils are asked to link a series of mimed activites imaginatively and a prize is given for the best effort.

(c) Memory and word games

These games involve activities such as memorising a series of objects, events in a story etc. in order that they might be reproduced at a later stage. The ability to recall is incorporated into a game. The stimulus may be pictorial, written or heard on a tape, and the recall element of the game may be structured in a variety of ways: pupils may be asked to write down the complete series; to call out the next in a series; to reconstruct a complete report including as many details as possible. The latter gives a meaningful, relevant purpose to a listening activity.

Word games may range from word associations, odd-one-out, word creations to variations of *Call My Bluff* in the foreign language, whereby a dictionary is used to provide evocative and interesting words for which the pupils have to provide three false definitions and one true, depending on the size of the group.

(d) Story games

This is an activity which we have mentioned under other categories: it involves the construction of a story by various means. One method is simply to provide an initial stimulus, perhaps a picture, which the first pupil uses to initiate the story. At a given signal the next pupil must pick up the story and continue it. This may be constructed as a group activity, and the final product could appear in written form to be read out for class amusement. It is a useful means of providing situations in which sentence structure and its associated problems are isolated and identified. The teacher may then decide to point out certain structural aspects of the language which pupils will need in order to complete the activity successfully.

These examples of games activities will no doubt suggest alternatives and variations which the teacher may wish to use. Wright Betteridge and Buckby in their book, *Games for Language Learning*, provide many more. One may prefer to adapt games one has enjoyed at parties to exploit their potential in the foreign language classroom. Indeed, it is possible to convert almost any activity into a game by, perhaps, introducing a competitive element into an activity which might otherwise be described as a 'test' and suggesting that boys compete against girls, or in the less sexist classrooms names A–M versus names N–Z! Instead of merely practising directions in the hypothetical street, a teacher might perhaps allow pupils to give direction to another pupil's home and all have to guess who is the occupant of that house.

Games, therefore, should have four functions:

1. to provide a reason for meaningful communication whilst pupils are participating in an activity with deliberate constraints
2. to deflect the interest of the participant from the language to the activity (we have already pointed out that the teacher's role is to direct the activity or the pupils' attention towards aspects of the language in order to facilitate the activity)
3. to introduce a 'play element' and thus promote a positive environment for language acquisition
4. to provide a positive atmosphere for social interaction and communication by the pupils.

6 Methodology and resources

DEVOLVING RESPONSIBILITY

In a communicative activity, the pupils must have the confidence to bridge an information gap. This confidence can only be gained if appropriate methodology is used from the very start. In other words, their contribution must be seen as instrinsically valuable for the success of the activity. In the traditional classroom, pupil response has been inhibited by a close analysis of the language they are using. If the activity is to be genuinely communicative, then the pupils must be allowed the freedom to communicate at will, and the teacher must relinquish a degree of central control. In these changes of role, the teacher is devolving responsibility and control of the task in order to involve the pupils' interest and thus their motivation.

Of course, attention must be focused on the language; it is no use expecting pupils to say or write something if they have not been equipped to do so. At the other extreme, it is very demotivating for pupils to be told that they are failing to express correctly something they had no interest in expressing in the first place! There must clearly be an appropriate balance between the medium and the message, so that interference by the teacher is either timed or structured in such a way that it does not inhibit the flow of communication and endanger the success of the interaction. The best language users will be those pupils who use the structures and lexis they have learnt formally as part of a pre-communicative activity to facilitate the interaction. Acquired competence then depends greatly on confidence and willingness to communicate in a variety of forms.

There are at least two ways of assessing a classroom linguistic activity: one can assess the performance in terms of its accuracy or its communicative effectiveness. Both of these features are obviously inextricably linked, but pupils become the arbiters of the communicative effectiveness of an utterance. The measure of success of an interchange is assessable in the comprehension and response by both partners. Failure to communicate is not eternalised in a mark book but is easily remedied by a request for repetition or rephrasing of the utterance. Teachers themselves will have to retain responsibility for assessing accuracy and effectiveness, although this need not always be carried out formally. It is more appropriate, given the integrated nature of communication, to assess its linguistic effectiveness during the activity, rather than summatively and discretely.

Progression through a language course to GCSE represents the transition from teacher dominance of the activity, through structured practice, to eventual pupil autonomy. That autonomy increases as the teacher dominance diminishes and, in the latter stages of a well-constructed course, the pupil will have gained the confidence and competence to perform autonomously in all four language skills. This progression from teacher dominance to pupil autonomy should be a conscious strategy by the teacher, and the classroom methodology should reflect this strategy. Confidence and competence cannot suddenly be expected to appear if they have not been carefully nurtured in the 'nursery' phrase of language learning and acquisition.

A vital ingredient of this growing confidence and sense of security is the use by the teacher of the target language. Pupils should quickly become familiar with hearing that language in order to develop their aural competence and pronunciation at an early stage. They may not be expected to respond immediately with accuracy and in complete sentences, but they should at least be surrounded by the target language as the prime medium of communication. At an elementary level they may only be expected to comprehend a simple question, answer in the affirmative or negative or select from a choice of two or three possibles to signal comprehension. The use of the target language for classroom administration, for instance, provides a valuable resource for giving and carrying out instructions, the introduction of everyday vocabulary and interpersonal or socialising talk. If the teacher remains consistent and perseveres in responding with the target language even when the pupils do not, then there will be an eventual acceptance of this language as a vehicle for communication. As a principle, it raises the status of the target language if it is perceived by the pupils as a functioning alternative to their own.

For the same reason there will have to be an equivalent adjustment in the traditional attitude to error in written or spoken language. Teachers automatically reach for red pens (or their oral counterpart!) when they read or hear a pupil's incorrect past participle, agreement or verb ending. Correcting error is a vital aspect of language teaching, and a communicative approach does not entail a casual attitude towards the error. The correction of error is, however, no longer the sole outcome of a linguistic activity if that activity is to have an interest, purpose and life of its own. The correction of error will now function at both conscious and subconscious levels, in precisely the same way as it does with first-language acquisition, where error correction is either spontaneous or controlled, depending on the situation, and is an integral part of the language acquisition process. That is what we shall have to emulate in our classrooms. Teachers are aware that many pupils are notoriously lax in seeing or hearing their own mistakes but they ought, perhaps, to be trained to see or hear error or, indeed, to identify error in the work of others. The responsibility for error correction is therefore no longer the sole property of the teacher, but, with pupils helping other pupils, it becomes an integral part of the effective communication process.

ASSESSMENT

The GCSE entails a reappraisal of traditional forms of assessment, and the chosen examination consortium plus the national criteria will influence the form of assessment within the classroom. The demand for communicative and purposeful activity adds a further dimension to the assessment process. The success of the outcome must be considered in evaluating the pupils' input. To this must be added the conflicting demands of an integrated-skill approach as opposed to discrete-skill assessment at GCSE. The demands of national criteria require the four skills to be tested separately, weighted equally and then combined to form an overall grade, but this may not be entirely compatible with language used communicatively or purposefully.

Teachers may be forgiven for merely switching to a form of assessment which reflects the GCSE pattern of differentiated objectives for the four language skills. In previous chapters we have suggested techniques for doing so quickly and accurately during classroom activities, but these can be adapted to assessing performance in integrated as well as discrete skills. These techniques are designed not to interfere unduly with the flow of communication. Yet more sophisticated criteria than those required for GCSE ought to be taken into account. Later we shall look forward to ways in which language teachers might raise the sophistication of their differentiated objectives to include criteria such as the ability to process factual information from the foreign language, or the ability to present personal information in the foreign language. Teacher expectations and classroom organisation will have to be adjusted accordingly. Both practising and student teachers will need training, not necessarily in mixed-group teaching, but in mixed-skill teaching with assessment using differentiated objectives and criteria.

CLASSROOM MANAGEMENT

The types of activity we have described will clearly require alternatives to a traditional concept of classroom management. A didactic style of teaching with mainly teacher/pupil interaction will have to yield to a less formal classroom structure which encourages pupil-to-pupil communication, either individually or in groups. We have already mentioned that the teacher as 'instructor' will have to increase his or her classroom functions to include that of 'facilitator'. This means assessing performance, resourcing activity, evaluating processes and being an administrator! As pupils become more familiar with this type of activity, they will take over some of these functions. By making resources readily available, a well-trained group will be able to resource and organise its own activities, if it is taught how to do so and if this is part of the classroom expectation from the elementary stages. Classroom organisation becomes of prime importance, as we can learn from good primary-school practice. The teacher will then be freed to carry out the functions for which he or she is qualified.

The physical environment is a vital consideration if our communicative activity is to succeed. Serried ranks of desks with the teacher positioned in front of a blackboard are not conducive to the type of communication we now expect, although a didactic methodology may be appropriate at certain times. Flexibility is called for, so that the teacher can alter the classroom environment according to the needs of a particular activity. This may require tables clustered for a particular group activity, lined up for a panel interview, pushed to the side so that pair-work can be effected, or set to the side of the pupils and chairs directed towards a focus or teacher-directed activity. Many classrooms and timetables present serious organisational obstacles for such a variety of approaches, but the key to solving such problems is the imagination and commitment of the teacher. Even a seemingly adverse classroom environment or the obstacle of a malignant timetable will yield some flexibility in the face of imagination and commitment.

One flexible classroom layout is to position the desks in groups or singly round the outside of the room, leaving the centre free for siting resources or for a role-play activity (Fig. 1). This central table or group of tables allows for greater access by pupils if they need to collect resources, rather than having to work their way between rows of desks. If a group needs to be isolated for remedial or extension work with the teacher, this can easily be carried out at this table without disrupting other activities in the classroom. The central table can be moved to one end to allow more space for role-play activities, and chairs need only to be reversed if the teacher wants class attention for

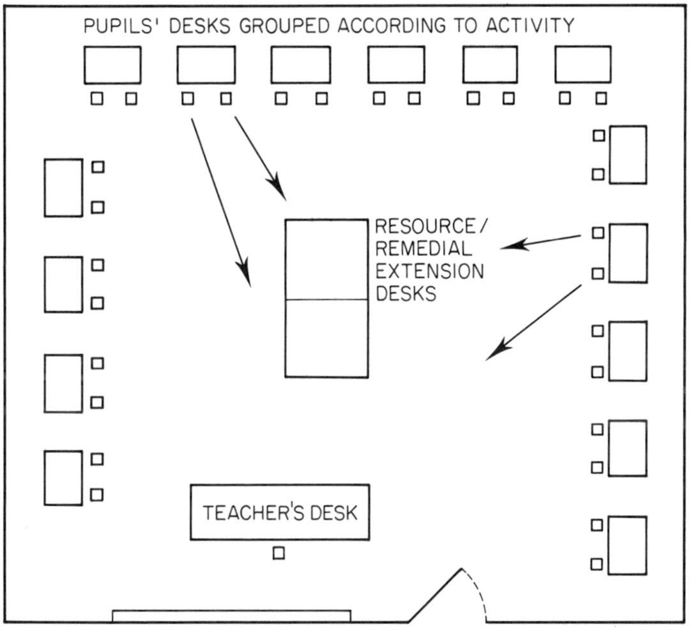

▲ *Fig. 1 A possible classroom layout*

explanation, instruction or clarification. If this layout is impossible, variations such as grouping tables round the outside of the classroom should also be considered. It is the work of moments for a well-disciplined class to change the structure of a classroom or return it to its original state and, if it improves pupil participation and performance, those moments will pay dividends throughout the lesson.

Thus the type of activity will dictate both the teacher's role and classroom formation. The pupils' performance and involvement will be enhanced as their participation and interest increase and therefore it is essential for pupils to feel confident and uninhibited in the foreign tongue. It may be that much pupil expression is not for teacher scrutiny. To take a simple information gap exercise as an example it may not be appropriate for the whole class or the teacher to be privy to the information which a single pupil has gained. It may only be necessary for the pupil to process that information or use it as data for a survey. It is the process which is more important than the product.

PUPIL TRANSITION TO COMPETENCE

In the traditional classroom, pupils progressed to a 'control' of the structure and lexis of the foreign language by means of teachers' explanations, usually in the mother tongue. In the 'communicative' classroom, pupils are expected to progress to competence with the help of teacher talk in the foreign language and authentic materials as their models. This expectation is not without is own inherent difficulties, particularly in the early stages. Pupils in the early stages of language acquisition inevitably lack the structures and vocabulary they need to participate in even the most elementary activities. The teacher must implant the structures and lexis necessary to a particular task. Activities at this level have to be carefully resourced and structured, so that pupils do not become disheartened. Modern research and experiment is particularly helpful here. Krashen and Terrell state in their Input Hypothesis that

> ..... we acquire (not learn) language by understanding input that is a little beyond our current level of (acquired) competence ... How do acquirers do this? How can we understand language that contains structures that we have not yet acquired? The answer is through context and extra-linguistic information. Good second language teachers do this by adding visual aids, by using extra-linguistic context. The input hypothesis thus claims that we use meaning to help us acquire language.

In the early stages of language acquisition we should surround pupils with the context for acquiring language, even if their language production or comprehension are not quite at that level. Krashen suggests that acquirers will go through a 'silent period' before launching into active language. Experiments in Canada have allowed pupils to respond in their mother tongue during that phase whilst remaining absolutely consistent with teacher-talk in the foreign tongue in all classroom transactions. Pupils then make the transition from the acquisitve stage to the productive stage when they are confident and ready.

What practical implications does this have for the teacher in the GCSE classroom? At an early stage it means that the teacher may not insist on total foreign language production by the pupils, since communication is effected even if the teacher uses the target language and the pupils respond in their mother tongue or by actions. In later stages of language-learning, the pupils should still be subjected to the foreign tongue and encouraged to use synonyms or alternative structures when the required structure or vocabulary do not come to mind.

Acceptance of alternatives in the interests of communication is a central tenet of the argument for a more communicative approach. In the classroom, the medium and the message have to be sensitively balanced by the teacher. Pupils still have to master, for instance, the past tense in order to describe an action in the past. The communication cannot take place without the linguistic medium. The teacher must remember, however, that learning structure should not be regarded as an *end* in itself but rather a *means* to a communicative end. Pupils may survive in the foreign language without mastering a particular grammatical structure, and they may even develop linguistic strategies for avoiding it, but there is no doubt that communication will be greatly enriched if they are able to manipulate such a structure in the appropriate situations.

EXPLOITATION OF TEXTS

A written or heard text may be exploited not only intensively but also extensively. Not every linguistic gem need be extracted from a text in order to broaden the pupils' fund of vocabulary and structure. Instead of doing what amounts to a virtual translation exercise, pupils will be expected to extract and process information for their own purposes. Languages will be absorbed more positively when there exists a perceived need for that language. In practical terms, this means that the texts must be authentic and relevant to the pupils' requirements in a given situation.

Research has shown that meaning is extracted in a variety of ways but is not wholly dependent on comprehending every element within a message. Provided the message holds an intrinsic interest for the recipient, then that person will use both semantic and syntactic strategies to glean the required information. This may require covering a wide range of material or close concentration on a single text. It may require extraction of individual pieces of information for use elsewhere or gaining an overview of the import of a text in what Krashen refers to as scanning and skimming.

In the classroom this will mean that questions related to a written or an aural source will concentrate not only on comprehension aspects but also on the more communicative activity of using that information for a second purpose. Thus, texts advertising different hotels might be used for comparison purposes by a pupil who has been given the role of a travel agent, having to balance conflicting demands by customers and hotel owners in order to arrive at an eventual solution.

That is an example of using a written text purposefully. A similar technique may be applied to a listening text, whereby pupils are expected to compare radio announcements for local entertainment in order to make a selection for a group of visitors. The effectiveness of the activity will depend entirely on the interest and involvement of the participants. The ingenuity of the teacher has to direct itself more towards ensuring that there is a genuine purpose in reading or listening. The content and the use made of the language will therefore become the most important consideration in selecting texts when the focus of attention is shifted from the form to the message.

AUTHENTIC MATERIALS

The *National Criteria* demand quite clearly that 'The basic principle is that the tasks set in the examination should be, as far as possible, authentic and valuable outside the classroom' (Para. 6.1). This is an admirable principle, but it needs the rigour of a closer inspection if one is successfully to translate its implications into classroom practice. For instance, can language divided into discrete skills, as is demanded elsewhere in the *National Criteria*, ever claim to be authentic? What precisely is meant therefore by the term 'authentic' in the context of the GCSE examination and in the context of our classroom materials? Widdowson draws an illuminating distinction between 'genuineness' and 'authenticity':

> Genuineness is a characteristic of the passage itself and is an absolute quality. Authenticity is a characteristic of the relationship between the passage and the reader and it has to do with appropriate response ... One of the problems, then, of presenting reading passages in the form of extracts, is that, though genuine enough, they may not engage the learner's attention in such a way as to render these authentic.

Authenticity cannot, therefore, be seen as divorced from the communicative activity it is resourcing. Arguably, any expression produced by a native speaker for the purpose of communication can be said to be authentic. As Dunning pointed out (SEC, Grade Related Criteria Working Party, 1985), the problem does not stop there. In discussing authenticity in examinations he writes:

> ... the question is *not* whether the candidates would ever be likely to find themselves in just such a situation, but rather is the task framed in such a way that the candidates' responses would enable one reasonably to infer whether or not, and to what degree, in any real life context making similar demands, the candidates would or would not show competence.

In our lessons we should therefore aim to create situations which use genuine or quasi-genuine materials for 'authentic' purposes. As teachers, we understand that learning and assessing modern languages in the classroom can never become totally genuine or authentic, since they are conscious and intentional activities with a specific linguistic focus. It is therefore the purpose to which the language is put in the classroom which will measure the degree of authenticity. The task set in the classroom should reflect the purposes for which the language was originally used.

Let us look at the use of a television news broadcast or documentary as an example of authenticity. Clearly, the material meets the primary criterion of genuineness. How does the teacher now ensure that its use is authentic? At an elementary level, the volume might be turned down and the teacher controls the language by asking questions about the scenes pupils are witnessing or by playing observation games in the foreign language. It is vital that the text is suitably short and that pupils' interest is focused on specifics. At GCSE level, the teacher must gauge the activity according to the ability of the class. A bottom set might watch and then comment in English, suggest sub-titles in either the foreign language or English, or complete a gap-filling text based on the transcript. A top set or post-GCSE group might do all these activities, then study the transcript, discuss the issues in the foreign language and finally produce their own televised news broadcast based on topical, local or school events to be viewed in a partner school or twinned town. Many schools now have video cameras which can be used for modern languages, not just for other subject areas.

If one were constructing a language module around such a broadcast and aiming eventually to use video cameras to produce scenes and commentary in the foreign language, there is a need for preparatory work to which pupils of varying abilities can contribute. Phrases and expressions will have to be gleaned from many broadcasts. Tapescripts, subtitles and commentaries will have to be produced, discussed and modified. All pupils will become involved in valid and valuable tasks.

The teacher might, however, feel that a particular text is better dealt with by the class as a unit for comprehension purposes. The intensive study of a written or heard text or dialogue can be regarded as an important stage along the path of language learning. However, when the text has been acquired, there must be a transition to its application in a purposeful and communicative activity.

RESOURCES

The methodology we have suggested will require appropriate resources, and we shall list below what these resources might include and suitable ways of deploying them. It is important to train pupils how to use the resource material available, on their own, during a particular activity.

Teacher

The teacher is obviously a most valuable resource. We have suggested that the teacher's role will become less didactic and more diversified as he or she takes over the roles of facilitator, enthusiastic language model, controller, assessor, participant and source of reference. This is clearly more demanding than the traditional language teacher's role and one which requires, above all, meticulous classroom management. At the same time, the organisational aspects must not become dominant if the pupils are not to lose sight of the primary objectives of the learning of modern languages.

Pupils

It is very easy to regard pupils merely as the recipients of language when they are, in fact, a valuable resource in the classroom. For language to function purposefully, it is imperative that the pupils themselves be exploited as the medium through which language can function. Pupils can be organised as the activity demands into groups, pairs, individuals, panels, performers, interrogators, reporters – the list is endless, and all permutations are potentially productive for pupils and teachers. It must be remembered that each pupil is an individual and brings, with him or her, their imagination, experience, ideas and personality to the activity, all of which influence the response of others in the group and the outcome.

Time

The allocation of time must be adequate for the task of language acquistion. Traditionally, teachers have preferred frequent but short sessions in order to reinforce learnt structures and vocabulary on a regular basis. The move towards a modular, experiential approach to language acquisition might suggest that longer, blocked periods on the timetable might be more flexible, effective and productive. Every school will have its own constraints and demands on curriculum time, and the final result is likely to be a compromise between expediency and ideal practice. However, larger time-blocks are more productive for communicative activities, allowing more work to be finished, and have the potential for more efficient language learning, although needing a high degree of classroom organisation.

Classroom

One of the obstacles to effective language teaching most frequently cited by teachers is accommodation. Yet it remains a vital resource. The ideal is for each individual language teacher to have a single classroom and be surrounded with all the resources for a whole range of activities. We have suggested ways in which the classroom layout might be improved. An environment must be provided that will stimulate activity and the exchange of language. Pupils need to be surrounded by readily transportable realia and works of reference.

Display is also of the utmost importance, since it reinforces learning and transmits messages about the language and the country where it is spoken. Not only walls but windows and ceilings can be used. Vocabulary and structural reinforcement can be done with the aid of word-mobiles, while pictures provide a visual stimulus. Pupils' work should also be prominent, giving an importance to their efforts.

It may be that a linguistic activity is more effectively carried out in a drama workshop, the school hall or field, or indeed in town. The seriousness and status of the activity in pupils' eyes are commensurate with the effort and imagination that have gone into its preparation. The environment should not be regarded, therefore, as an obstacle but as an opportunity.

The assistant

Another important resource for language activity is the assistant. Although an endangered species in certain LEAs their function can sometimes be substituted or supplemented by exchange students or visitors from abroad. Their presence must be exploited by teachers and pupils alike as an opportunity to experience a source of authentic language. To use them merely to practise oral questions prior to the examination is not to realise their full potential. They should be fully incorporated into the full range of linguistic activities and exploited as a source of reference. They can clearly influence the activities in classes at all levels.

Just as the teacher's role has become greatly diversified, that of the assistant will become one of supporting enabler. They will be to monitor and participate in the varying types of activities in the 'communicative' classroom. The teacher might decide to control and evaluate the process, leaving the assistant to provide the linguistic core of the situation. It is most important that assistants are well briefed and prepared by the teacher before lessons.

However, working in the classroom is not the only means of support an assistant can give – they may, at times, be better used in preparing materials for the teachers. Assistants can be relied upon to produce or to help produce taped or written texts of various types. Thus, just as the teachers will have to diversify their role, so too will the assistants.

Coursebook

A single coursebook cannot hope to provide the far wider range of linguistic experience now expected at GCSE level. To follow a coursebook slavishly would negate all efforts towards genuine communicative activity, although such books may well provide much source material and a multitude of ideas and suggestions for exploiting that material communicatively. It is the teacher's responsibility to control the flow of communication by using the coursebook to support the activities he or she chooses.

There may well be parts of certain books which are ideally

suited to a module being undertaken in the classroom. The teacher must have these tabulated and categorised. The school's computers might have an important part to play in storing the information to be used in constructing a unit or module. All the material the department possesses as part of coursebooks, worksheets, OHP transparencies, realia, video and taped material could then be categorised and filed in the computer for use in the construction of modules later.

Dictionaries

The use of dictionaries has been actively discouraged in many classrooms and in most examinations in recent years. GCSE, regrettably, will not change that situation overnight. We believe that dictionaries *do* have a place in any communicative activity. All teachers of modern languages are aware of the dangers of their misuse which are often cited as a justification for banning them. The use of dictionaries should, however, be controlled and practised from the early stages, so that pupils will use them correctly as an added source of reference for many classroom activities.

Realia

A vital accessory for any module which is planned to practise language directed towards a particular theme will be a well-stocked and well-catalogued realia store. If a teacher is based in a single room, he or she may wish to make such items readily available around the classroom as a language stimulus. They include brochures, posters, timetables, advertisements, letters (formal and informal), menus, packets, labels, games, records, audio-tapes, video-tapes, newspapers, magazines, pamphlets, handouts, programmes, bills, receipts, tickets, maps, recipes, signs – the list in itself is virtually endless.

This cornucopia of material presents the teacher with three problems: collecting, cataloguing and exploitation. The primary source for collecting realia is clearly the foreign country in question. Any links via the school, the twinned town, social contacts or merely a friend on holiday should immediately be exploited for realia. Most of these objects have little more than souvenir value for the individual, but vast potential for the classroom. Once an exchange school, for instance, is aware of what is useful for classroom purposes, the tide of realia can overwhelm the receiving school!

Listening and reading texts will have to be selected, evaluated and processed for classroom use in a variety of acitvities. Publishers are aware of the need for this type of material, and it is becoming available on the market, in part at least. However, texts by their nature rarely remain up-to-date, topical and commercially viable at the same time. The answer may well be the setting up of county or LEA resource banks to which individual schools can contribute and from which they can draw.

The solution of a centralised resource bank would save the

multiplication of effort necessary if each school is to categorise and catalogue the material it has available. All material gathered must be catalogued for classroom use in a range of classroom activities. It may well be that the computer has a role here. Then, if teachers are planning particular modules, they must simply check their requirements, order the material and have it available in the classroom during the course or unit. Schools may prefer, however, to have their own resource bank more readily available, catalogued with the aid of a chart.

Catalogued resource banks will leave the teachers free to concentrate on exploiting the available material in the classroom. This will depend largely on the activity. Letters received from the exchange school in real handwriting will provide practice in reading and replying at different levels. This is now a requirement for GCSE. Once the activity had been defined and pupils are aware of what they have available in the way of resources, they themselves will be able to collaborate on its exploitation.

Audio-visual equipment and computers

All the equipment traditionally associated with work in the modern-language classroom will have equal, of not greater, importance in the communicative activities we described. Radio and television will remain a source of authentic material, whilst audio and video recording will provide alternative material modes of presentation of material. Pupils always take greater care with a role play or interview if they know it is to be recorded over a microphone or with a camera. This will help to raise the status of the linguistic activity still further and provide useful organisational skills for pupils to master. Teachers may wish to consider the recording of short plays, poems or radio and television 'reports' written by pupils.

This equipment should be put at the disposal of pupils as far as possible, so that they are not compelled to rely on a written presentation of all the language they produce. Thus, one suggested activity might require pupils to describe to a group the photographs they have taken and presented with a slide projector. The overhead projector and transparencies might serve a similar function.

Computers are still in their infancy in the modern languages classroom, with too many electronic Banda sheets, but as the software improves in sophistication so too will its usefulness. Pupils can be encouraged to use computers in order to store or present linguistic information. Provided the problem of access to keyboard and monitor can be overcome, computer-assisted learning has great potential for pupils and modern languages on an individual or small-group basis. Although the computer is not in itself flexible and open-ended enough for genuine communication to take place, it nevertheless provides a useful resource for extension or remedial language work.

7 Future trends

POTENTIAL FOR CHANGE

Curriculum development is organic in character and changes according to pupils', and society's, needs. There are, occasionally, major thrusts in this development, such as the GCSE, which sweep away old attitudes and instigate major changes, which are then formalised through documents and structures such as syllabuses and examinations. However, once formalised, it does not mean that change and adaptation cannot or should not continue to take place. All developments must be looked at with a critical eye. To this end, the Secondary Examinations Council is responsible not only for ensuring that examination schemes conform to the national criteria, but also for reviewing those criteria themselves, and advising on possible extensions and changes. The GCSE *General Criteria* (para. 6) make this quite clear and continue to say,

> The Council will also be able to make recommendations to the Secretaries of State for temporary dispensations from individual provisions of the National Criteria where the Council is satisfied that this is necessary in order that promising innovations in syllabuses or assessment procedures may be tested.

This means that, even now, new ideas can be put forward, new approaches suggested, even if they do not wholly conform to the national criteria, allowing for such developments as modular coursework based schemes. This chapter tries to pinpoint some of these developments, and looks forward to possible innovations in the coming decade.

GRADE CRITERIA

In order to give some indication of the level of attainment reached by candidates obtaining particular grades, the national criteria, at present, offer grade descriptions for grades F and C. These are, however, very generalised statements and give but limited help in showing what a candidate with a specific grade can do. Therefore, it is intended to extend the national criteria by including a more objective system of criteria-related grading. That is to say, each grade would be closely defined in terms of what a candidate would be expected to do in order to gain a particular grade. The *GCSE: A General Introduction* document states:

> With the new system of criteria-related grading, grades awarded will be based more closely on recognised standards and defined levels of attainment . . . the National Criteria will be extended to include grade criteria, which will define the main areas of knowledge and understanding and the main skills and competences within each subject which the examinations will be

designed to test and the levels of attainment which candidates will be expected to demonstrate in each of these if they are to be awarded particular grades.

The Secondary Examinations Council, accordingly, set up working parties to produce draft grade criteria in a range of subjects. The French group's proposals were finalised in the summer of 1985, and subsequently a German group was established which reported in the winter of 1986. The General Introduction (para. 31) makes it clear that 'the Government attaches great importance to the introduction of criteria-related grading and grade criteria'. It was intended that these criteria should be implemented by 1990, but, as little has happened since the publication of the draft proposals, that date would now appear unlikely. Hopefully they will finally become part of the national criteria, otherwise a great deal of time, expertise and money will have been wasted.

The grade criteria for French set out to devise a system which will:

- set clear goals to help motivate and stretch pupils of all abilities
- encourage and reward mastery of specified levels of competence
- make clear the meaning of grades, in terms of attainment, to all users (e.g. pupils, teachers, employers, further and higher education).

Grade criteria have continued the approach of the national criteria by taking the four domains of listening, reading, speaking and writing, and then defining seven areas of competence within each domain. These areas of competence (AoC) correspond to the seven overall grades (A–G), with AoCs 1–4 covering the basic skills and 5–7 matching the higher level. Within each AoC, the required competences are clearly defined and, from AoC1, the lowest competence, each AoC builds upon the previous one, in ascending order of difficulty. Candidates have to show mastery in each AoC to gain a point, and to do this, they must complete satisfactorily 70 per cent of the tasks set. The points would then be aggregated, and from this total the final grade would be determined. An example of the competence definitions for one domain is given in Figure 1.

The grade criteria also place an emphasis on the development of mixed skill teaching and coursework. The German criteria follow a broadly similar pattern to the French, but have chosen only four AoCs rather than seven, and place greater emphasis on mixed skills and coursework. It is probably an improvement to reduce the number of AoCs to four, since the French criteria system has been criticised as likely to be unwieldy. Criticism has also been made about their prescriptive nature, which could possibly block experimentation and also make examination setting difficult.

▼ *Fig. 1 Competence definitions for listening*

	BASIC LEVEL			
	RESTRICTED RANGE (8 topics and settings)		FULL BASIC RANGE (10–12 topics and settings)	
	AREA OF COMPETENCE 1	AREA OF COMPETENCE 2	AREA OF COMPETENCE 3	AREA OF COMPETENCE 4
Candidates are able to ...	... listen to and understand important points and details in short instructions, announcements and requests in French.	... listen to and understand specific details in short dialogues in French.	... listen to and understand important points and details in instructions, announcements and requests in French.	... listen to and understand specific details in interviews and monologues (e.g. weather forecasts) in French.

HIGHER LEVEL		
TOTAL RANGE (approx. 14 topics and settings)		
AREA OF COMPETENCE 5	AREA OF COMPETENCE 6	AREA OF COMPETENCE 7
... identify themes and details in anouncements, instructions, requests, interview and dialogues in French.	... identify themes and details (including attitudes, ideas and emotions) in announcements, instructions, requests, interviews and dialogues in French.	... draw conclusions from and see relations within extended announcements, instructions, requests, interviews and dialogues in French.

However, these criticisms can be overcome, and the implementation of grade criteria can only strengthen the GCSE examination for modern languages. It would make the examination completely criterion-referenced and would strengthen the emphasis on practical communication and on the use of authentic tests and relevant tasks. Because each AoC is defined in terms of what a pupil can do, then the final overall grade becomes a positive statement of attainment, at whatever level; this means that the lower grades, as well as the higher, have an intrinsic value and are worth having, rather than being considered failure. This must be good for languages!

COURSEWORK

The various reasons for coursework were outlined in Chapter 1, and many times throughout the book instances have been given where coursework would provide a more integrated approach and a fairer mode of assessment than traditional examinations. It allows mixed-skill testing in more 'authentic' linguistic situations. More interesting work of an extended nature can be undertaken, giving pupils the possibility of sifting, collecting and collating information in the foreign language, and then using this in different forms of oral or written work. It is, therefore, a valid compromise of an assessment model, and its virtual exclusion from GCSE modern languages must be remedied.

Coursework is a form of continuous assessment, and this can present a certain problem to teachers, since there are two kinds of assessment needed: the formal or structured and the informal or unstructured. The informal or unstructured form is more subjective in nature and will be used in a mixed-skill situation to assess process. This will be difficult to accomplish, i.e. the teacher must know what he or she is looking for. The assessment objectives must be clear. The formal or structured assessment tends to be discrete-skill and task-based. It assesses whether the task has been done and the degree of competence in the quality of performance.

Both forms of assessment should be used for coursework, to evaluate the process during a project and to assess the outcome at the end, or several outcomes within the project. Pupils working in groups discussing, expressing opinions, eliciting information can be assessed informally, while the follow-up, writing a letter, making a wall-chart, recording a dialogue, can be tested formally. However, to assess continuously needs practice, both for teacher and pupil. Such techniques cannot start in year 4, but ought to be implemented from year 1.

An important implication of coursework for the classroom is one of time. Language teachers have tended to espouse the drip-feed theory, wanting short, regular periods of time throughout the week. This, however, is becoming less and less defensible. Developments in the curriculum are leading towards timetabling in long blocks of time, and languages can fit into this pattern. A 35-minute period is, in reality, one of 25 minutes in terms of work time, and very little can be completed in this time; this certainly is not conducive to good coursework. Languages should be looking towards extended periods of time, perhaps a whole morning, so that intensive work can be done. Experience in Wiltshire has shown that pupils enjoy intensive language work, and in those few schools who have tried a whole morning it has been found that time goes by quickly, pupils get invloved in their work and a good deal of ground can be covered. If a teacher is well organised and well prepared, the long block of time is not a hindrance but a help.

At present examination groups are looking at ways of including coursework into GCSE modern languages. Indeed, the SEG had a languages sub-committee which proposed the inclusion of up to 30 per cent coursework in the examination. This has yet to be implemented, and, although more research is necessary, ought not to be shelved. There are other projects to examine the possibility of Mode 3 examinations with a heavy, or complete, coursework content. It has been suggested that individual schools could make up their own course and assessment model as a Mode 3, so that an examination group's syllabus became merely a checklist to ensure that the requisite topics, settings and structures had been covered, thus giving freedom of approach. It is clear that competence in reading, listening and speaking cannot be adequately assessed in a half-hour's test, particularly when extensive reading is a requirement at higher level. Pupils should not be given only truncated extracts, but ought to have the satisfaction of tackling longer passages.

The developments in coursework are interesting and vital, and should be supported when they appear, particularly as the coursework approach fits in well with developments in both profiling and modular syllabuses.

PROFILING AND MODERN LANGUAGES

At a time when teachers of modern languages feel, quite justifiably, that their time and energies will be fully committed to the requirements of a new examination, it seems invidious to charge them with yet another consideration. Profiling is but a single important facet of a wide-ranging reformation of the curriculum, already underway, which will influence all teachers and teaching over the next decade. GCSE is also part of this reform and should contribute to a more experiential and process-orientated curriculum relying on more explicit and better documented forms of assessment. Moreover, the DES will require all schools to produce a complete Record of Achievement for each pupil by 1990:

i. *Recognition of achievement* Records and recording systems should recognise, acknowledge and give credit for what pupils have achieved and experienced, not just in terms of results in public examinations but in other ways as well. They should do justice to pupils' own efforts and to the efforts of teachers, parents, ratepayers and taxpayers to give them a good education.
ii. *Motivation and personal development* They should contribute to pupils' personal development and progress by improving their motivation, providing encouragement and increasing their awareness of strengths, weaknesses and opportunities.
iii. *Curriculum and organisation* The recording process should help schools to identify the all-round potential of their pupils and to consider how well their curriculum teaching and organisation enable pupils to develop the general, practical and social skills which are to be recorded.

(*Records of Achievement: a statement of policy*, DES, 1986)

Departments of modern languages will naturally be expected to contribute to this record of achievement for each pupil. When they do so, they must scrutinise precisely what pupils have attained in the way of positive achievements in each language area. Within a few years it will no longer be acceptable merely to quote an examination grade at 16 + as evidence of success or failure, since that grade conveys little information in itself to the outside world. Unless grade criteria are introduced, it remains a reference along a normative scale. Already the GCSE expects teachers to utilise differentiated internal assessment results in deciding on the entry pattern for all pupils. In certain examinations groups, the decision has been made to report performance in all four discrete skills, showing how the final global grade was obtained. Only the final grade, however, will appear on the certificate. This is a simple profile!

Since teachers should record evidence of a pupil's performance in the four skill areas in order to justify entry at a given level for GCSE, it is only a small step for them to record evidence of performance in a variety of other skills and achievements, not usually assessed discretely, but nevertheless taken into consideration when marking a pupil's oral or written contribution. These might include fluency, use of idiom or ability to initiate conversation.

The idea of a pupil profile is that it not only provides the assessment criteria by which a pupil's performance is judged, but also that it should provide the basis for regular discussions between teacher and pupil, leading to the identification of strengths and weaknesses and, hopefully an improvement of performance.

What form should this profile take in the case of modern languages? Many teachers, having to provide evidence of performance in the four skill areas in order to support the entry pattern for each pupil at GCSE, are recording an assessment divided into discrete skills in their mark books. This is, indeed, an improvement on an assessment pattern whose criteria were often unclear.

It is also no longer sufficient to say 'could do better' or 'must work harder' without defining how and in which aspects of language work that performance may be improved. The teaching objectives for each stage and level of language learning will be set out in departmental or faculty schemes of work. Thus, if a modern languages department considers that its middle sets in the third year should be able to write a simple letter giving personal information or that pupils should be fluent in basic social responses, then these should be included in the teaching and assessment programme.

Clearly, it is impossible to assess all teaching objectives in all four skills in every lesson or in every completed piece of written work. Indeed, it is not necessary to assess in every lesson or with every piece of written work; it does mean that when assessment takes place, the teacher must know what he or she is assessing, i.e. the objectives must be clear. This is why most teachers have resorted to a global grade for speed and convenience. However, it is demotivating for a pupil to receive a global grade D for their work when they are unsure of the assessment criteria. Teachers may then decide that, with a piece of written work or during the course of a certain classroom activity, only one or two aspects of pupils' linguistic performance will be assessed and recorded. This allows a profiled picture to be built up during a given time-span: a six-week module or term, for instance. The department must decide precisely what is being assessed and the criteria by which it should be assessed. The progress of each pupil may then be recorded on an individual sheet, as in Figure 2.

▼ *Fig. 2 A possible departmental profile*

NAME:					CLASS:		
		UNIT 1	UNIT 2	UNIT 3	UNIT 4	UNIT 5	UNIT 6
Listening	5						
	4						
	3	*		*	*	*	
	2		*				*
	1						
	0						
Speaking	5						*
	4					*	
	3				*		
	2			*			
	1	*	* *				
	0						
Reading	5						
	4						
	3				*		
	2		*	*		*	*
	1	* *					
	0						
Writing	5						
	4						
	3						
	2					*	
	1	*			*		* *
	0		*	*			
Use of Idiom	5						
	4						
	3						
	2				*		
	1	*	*	*		*	*
	0						
Fluency	5						
	4		*		*	*	*
	3	*		*			
	2						
	1						
	0						
Ability to Manipulate Structures	5						
	4						
	3						
	2						
	1	*				*	*
	0		*	*	* *		
Ability to Process and Present Inform. in Foreign Lang.	5						
	4						
	3				*	* *	
	2	*	*	*			*
	1						
	0						
	5						
	4						
	3						
	2						
	1						
	0						
Content and Objectives of Units							
Assessment Criteria for Group							

Obviously, the descriptors can be adapted or added to according to a department's priorities. The quality of performance can be judged on a predetermined scale such as the 0–5 scale described in Chapter 3. Also, not every descriptor is applicable to each unit, and within each unit, a descriptor may be assessed more than once.

In all probability, the minimum number of language skills to be assessed will be four, but departments may well identify more. If more than ten or twelve are selected, the assessment process is likely to become unwieldy and counter-productive. Pupils are likely to take more personal responsibility for their own progress if they are able to discuss this openly with teachers.

For this system to work efficently, teachers must have a clear understanding of the linguisitc objectives of all work undertaken as part of a unit. These objectives should be recorded in the scheme of work, which would also include details of the assessment criteria for each identifiable objective. When teachers are producing such assessment and criteria, or descriptors of performance, the level and ability of the group must be taken into account, so that the goals set are attainable for all pupils in that group. If all these factors are considered, a properly used profiling system could transform pupils' motivation, achievement and standards in modern-language classrooms. In providing more information to pupils, parents and employers, a profiling system can only be beneficial for modern languages.

MODERN LANGUAGES IN THE MODULAR CURRICULUM

Another aspect of the present reform of the curriculum is a move towards modular-based, more experiential learning. Again, GCSE may be seen as one step along the path away from the mere assimilation of facts and towards the understanding and experiencing of processes. Increasingly, schools will be expected to identify the skills and areas of experience with which their pupils will come into contact. They will then have to construct a curriculum which will best deliver the form of education they have indentified. This curriculum is more likely to be modular and/or integrated in form, since a valid area of educational experience cannot always be contained within the confines of a single subject. Technology, for instance, may rely on skills or areas of experience drawn from science and CDT faculties. 'Humanities' may be a more effective way of delivering what was traditionally taught within the subjects of geography, history and religious education. As the curriculum becomes increasingly flexible, units containing valid and valuable experience will be constructed in order that pupils may leave school with more identifiable skills.

A modular curriculum of this type presents a difficulty for teachers with traditional expectations of subject material and methodology, since it demands negotiable material and a less didactic approach to teaching. Teachers will have to be trained to cope with the implications of the increased flexibility demanded of them and the adjustment of role it may entail.

Languages, in the past, have been resistant to cross-curricular integration, but, if they are to survive and flourish as part of the more flexible and integrated core curriculum in the next decade, their exclusion from a modular approach would be educationally unjustifiable. Several groups are looking at the possibility of devising a modular scheme of assessment, such as that being developed under the auspices of the Future Curriculum Trends Committee of the SEG. Here there is a basic core of three modules to which can be added up to two more, giving access to the higher grades. Each module covers a range of topics at both basic and higher levels, includes work in all four skills and encourages mixed skill tasks and assessment. It may also include coursework and continuous assessment.

Examination groups are showing interest in unit accreditation, which could be a way forward beyond GCSE. Extension modules could be added to the GCSE in a range of options. There could be modules slanted towards business needs, while others might have a literary content or a leisure base. These could be put together in various ways leading to certification at AS or A level, a Foreign Languages at Work Certificate (London Chamber of Commerce) or an RSA qualification and would cover many linguistic needs in the 16–18 age-range. It would certainly allow languages to be offered to a greater number of pupils than at present in sixth forms and would also enable us to view languages across the whole 14–18 curriculum, again fitting in well with recent developments.

Chapter 1 discussed the importance of the graded test movement in the development of national criteria, and some groups – such as MEG – are looking at the feasibility of certificating different levels of these tests and finally incorporating them into GCSE; each level could be seen as a module and, with accreditation of these modules, we are looking at assessment from year 1 onwards, something which could give a flexibility and quite different aspect to the examination. Pupils could continue with a 'mainline' course straight through to the fifth year in one language, possibly starting a second on the way. They could, alternatively, take three modules at the end of third year, end their study of one language and start another one in the fourth year, to be awarded, finally, a certificate in foreign languages, with recorded attainment in both languages counting towards the final grade.

This, of course, would be possible now, since GCSE is not age-related. Those pupils who feel they have reached a plateau in French after three years could probably attempt basic level and maybe achieve a grade E. If they wished to continue language study, or if languages were in the core curriculum, they could then start German and take the basic level after two years' study, and possibly obtain another E. This would represent positive achievement for many pupils, as well as two certificates, and reflect the image of the enjoyment and satisfaction of walking up two, or even three, smaller hills rather than slogging away on the stony path to the top of a high mountain whose summit may never even come into sight. Limited, attainable goals are not to be seen as a lowering of standards, but the very opposite to those pupils for whom they are appropriate.

Finally, TVEI is another development into which languages can fit in modular form, although it must be emphasised that they should not be seen as an appendage to some other project base, but rather as important enough to stand on their own, or as an integral part of a complete unit. It must be remembered that TVEI is not a course, but more curriculum development with the added, considerable, incentive of substantial funding.

The money and small groups has enabled teachers to make rapid advances in methodology and approach. For example, in one school it has meant being able to equip every pupil in the group with a C60 cassette tape, and, instead of always taking home exercise books to mark, the teacher often takes home a box of tapes for assessment. Besides being a project base in its own right, languages can, as suggested, be an important part of a unit, as for example, on tourism. Here the pupil may well tackle aspects of history, geography, business studies and organisation skills, and a foreign language module, possibly incorporating the requirements for the basic-level core of reading, listening and speaking, would complete the picture.

CONCLUSION

This book, in trying to examine various aspects of the GCSE examination in modern languages, has underlined the fact that to prepare for the new examination is to consider and take on board considerable curriculum development in language teaching. It has also raised the point that the examination, although innovative and a considerable improvement on the previous system, has its weak spots and needs to be developed.

The GCSE is tending to be rather narrow in its approach and, even at higher level, very transactional. Authentic text types are certainly used, but have brought with them a wealth of accidents and robberies. The picture given of the world abroad is rather materialistic, and there seems to be little room for imagination. Imaginative writing is not only interesting for its own sake, but gives an idea of the national psyche, and in the fifth year, at higher level, pupils should be tackling this. It would also mean them using the foreign language for their own creative writing – and they certainly *can* write poems in French or German, or any other language, at this level.

The present national criteria stipulate that languages should be tested in four skill areas, and arguments have been presented in previous chapters against discrete skill testing. As all four skills are integrated across communicative activity, it might be sensible to redefine these four skill areas or domains, and situate the examination around other domains, not necessarily just four. There could be, for example, the following domains:

- The interpreter
- Transacting business of everyday life
- The world of work
- The world of leisure
- Understanding foreign culture (i.e. imaginative writing, listening – songs, poems, plays)

These domains could all be tested at basic and higher levels, and would fit all topic areas and settings, but would be mixed-skill, and may produce meaningful language and tasks for the learner. This is a development to look forward to.

However, although we may carp at the format and content of the examination, it must be admitted that it has also brought many good things. Above all, it has answered the need produced by developments outlined in Chapter 1, and the examination groups are, by and large, prepared to adapt, change and develop. The Secondary Examinations Council should, perhaps, take the lead in imaginative developments by at least offering positive support. There are many exciting areas to explore, such as the use of video for assessment purposes – and others have been outlined in the last chapter.

Van Humboldt was quoted by Dakin in *The Language Laboratory and Language Learning* as saying, 'We cannot teach a language; we can only create the conditions under which it will be learned.' This is more than ever true for us today, since the teacher, in a communicative approach, is becoming the facilitator of the learning environment. This means that materials and preparation are of paramount importance, more so than marking as traditionally done, and we must adjust our time and attitudes accordingly.

The one overriding aspect of the GCSE is that it has put as a priority the need to test and record positive achievements and, linked to this, placed the emphasis on practical skills and communication. This, in turn, has obliged teachers to examine carefully the methodology, aims and objectives of language teaching (see Figure 3).

The message, in terms of methodology, is that language needs a focus to develop motivation in learners. Language tasks in the classroon need a communicative purpose. With these developments in mind, the future for languages must be brighter than for a very long time, and the GCSE, with all its imperfections, is at the heart of these developments.

Figure 3 ▼

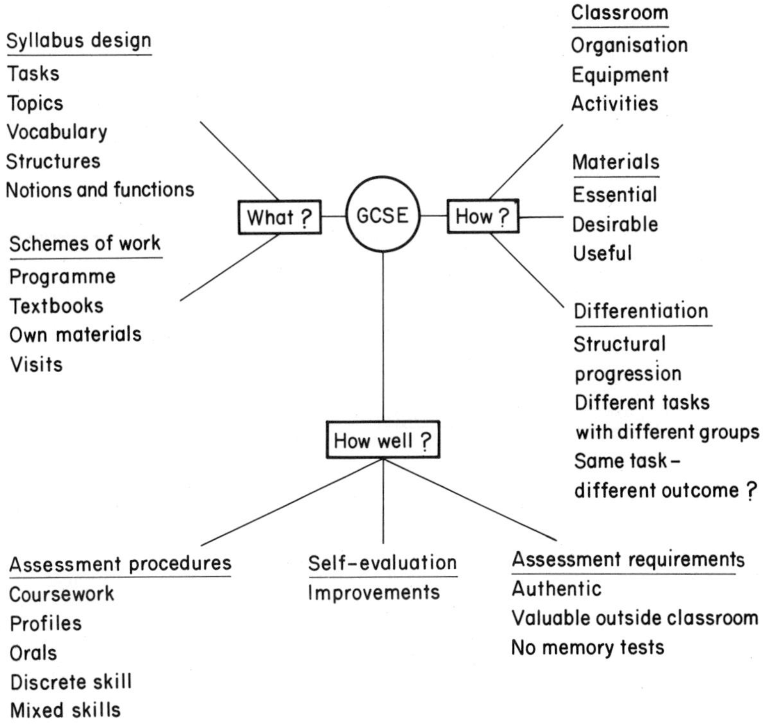
Syllabus design
Tasks
Topics
Vocabulary
Structures
Notions and functions
Schemes of work
Programme
Textbooks
Own materials
Visits
What ?
GCSE
How ?
Classroom
Organisation
Equipment
Activities
Materials
Essential
Desirable
Useful
Differentiation
Structural progression
Different tasks with different groups
Same task – different outcome ?
How well ?
Assessment procedures
Coursework
Profiles
Orals
Discrete skill
Mixed skills
Self-evaluation
Improvements
Assessment requirements
Authentic
Valuable outside classroom
No memory tests

Bibliography

Assessment of Performance Unit. *Foreign Language Performance in Schools, Report on 1983 Survey*. Published by the DES.

Brumfit and Johnson (1979) *The Communicative Approach to Language Teaching*, Oxford University Press.

Brumfit (1984) *Communicative Methodology in Language Teaching*, Cambridge University Press.

CILT (1981) *Directory of Organisations and Centres for Language Teachers*, CILT (also many other publications on tests, graded tests and communication).

Dakin (1973) *The Language Laboratory and Language Learning*, Longman.

DES (1985) *General Certificate of Secondary Education – A General Introduction*, HMSO.

DES (1985) *General Certificate of Secondary Education – The National Criteria, General Criteria*, HMSO.

DES (1985) *The Curriculum from 5–16 – Curriculum Matters 2*, HMI Series, HMSO.

Grellet (1981) *Developing Reading Skills*, Cambridge University Press.

Hawkins (1981) *Modern Languages in the Curriculum*, Cambridge University Press.

Johnson and Morrow (1981) *Communication in the Classroom*, Longman.

Klippel (1984) *Keep Talking*, Cambridge University Press.

Krashen (1982) *Principles and Practice in Second Languauge Acquisition*, Pergamon.

Krashen and Terrell (1983) *The Natural Approach*, Pergamon.

Littlewood (1981) *Communication Language Teaching*, Cambridge University Press.

Littlewood (1984) *Foreign and Second Language Learning*, Cambridge University Press.

Maley and Duff (1982) *Drama Techniques in Language Learning*, Cambridge University Press.

Morgan and Rinvolucri (1983) *Once Upon a Time*, Cambridge University Press.

Neuner, Krüger and Grewer (1981) *Übungstypologie zum kommunikativen Deutschunterricht*, Langenscheidt.

Pattison (1987) *Developing Communication Skills*, Cambridge University Press.

Secondary Examinations Council (1986) GCSE – *A Guide for Teachers: French*, Open University Press.

Secondary Examinations Council and BBC. *A Guide to the GCSE*, Broadcasting Support Services.

Service Compris, Mary Glasgow Publications, subscriptions order.

Ur (1981) *Discussions that Work*, Cambridge University Press.

Ur (1984) *Teaching Listening Comprehension*, Cambridge University Press.

Widdowson (1978) *Teaching Language as Communication*, Oxford University Press.

Wright, Betteridge and Buckby (1982) *Games for Language Learning*, 2nd edn, Cambridge University Press.